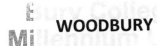

Practice in
German Grammar

for students starting post-16 courses

Second edition

Alan G Jones and
Gudrun Lawlor

First published in 1992 by:
Mary Glasgow Publications, an imprint of Stanley Thornes (Publishers) Ltd

This edition first published in 2001 by:
Nelson Thornes Ltd
Delta Place
27 Bath Road
CHELTENHAM
GL53 7TH
United Kingdom

09 / 10 9 8

A catalogue record for this book is available from the British Library.

ISBN 978 0 7487 5782 4

Ilustrations by Ian Heard
Edited by Sarah Provan
Page make-up by Tech-Set Ltd

Printed in China

The authors wish to acknowledge their indebtedness to:
- Professor Martin Durrell, whose Using German and revised editions of
  Hammer's German Grammar have proved particularly useful in the preparation
  of this book
- Collette Biggs for her help and encouragement with the first edition
- Gabriele Reinsch for reading through the second edition.

Contents

Using this book

Use this book to find out about and practise grammatical points that are causing you problems in your written or spoken German. You can work through it in sequence, or look up specific points as required.

○ Use the Index at the back of the book to find out where a particular point is explained and practised.

○ For each unit, study the dialogue at the start to find out how the grammatical structures covered are used in context. Use a dictionary to look up essential vocabulary. The phrases in bold print are explained and in most cases translated later in the unit.

○ Read the explanation of the grammar rules in English and make sure you fully understand them.

○ Learn by heart the German examples of each structure.

○ Test your understanding by doing the exercises linked to each section. Write out the whole sentence or passage rather than just the word or phrase asked for.

○ Check your answers with the correct version at the back of the book (pages 193-215). Pay particular attention to any you got wrong; re-read the rules to see why you got them wrong, and if you still cannot understand why, consult your teacher.

○ Most of the exercises are based on a limited vocabulary related to the dialogues. A few, however, are deliberately more wide-ranging to add interest.

○ Only learning by heart and frequent consolidation will enable you to fully master German grammatical structures so that you can use them confidently in your own written and spoken German.

○ As you read more German, you will become aware of variations in style which may diverge from some of the grammar 'rules'. Make a note of these, and discuss them with your teacher.

Glossary of grammatical terms

Nouns

○ A noun is a word used to name a person or an object or an abstract quality

ein **Student**	*a student*
eine **Schreibmaschine**	*a typewriter*
die **Schönheit**	*beauty*

○ In German all nouns are written with an initial capital letter.

○ Nouns may be masculine, neuter or feminine (***gender***), and they may be singular or plural (***number***).

Determiners

○ A ***determiner*** indicates which nouns you are talking about. There are various types of determiner.

○ Both German and English have a ***definite article:***

der, das, die   *the*

and an ***indefinite article:***

ein, eine   *a*

○ German also has a ***negative indefinite article:***

kein, keine   *not a*

○ ***Possessives*** indicate who the noun belongs to:

mein, meine   *my*
sein, seine   *his*

○ ***Demonstratives*** are words such as:

dieser, dieses, diese   *this*
jeder, jedes, jede   *every*

Adjectives

○ An **adjective** is a word used to describe a noun:

> ein **neuer** Rock   *a new skirt*
> der Anzug ist **teuer**   *the suit is expensive*

○ Adjectives may be **free-standing**:

> der Anzug ist **teuer**

or part of a **noun phrase**, i.e. they precede a noun:

> ein **neuer** Rock

When free-standing, German adjectives do not take endings; when part of a noun phrase, they take **primary endings** (e.g. ein neu**er** Rock) or **secondary endings** (e.g. der neu**e** Rock).

○ The **comparative** form of an adjective is used when making comparisons between two people or things:

> Der Rock ist **teurer**   *The skirt is more expensive*
> als die Bluse.   *than the blouse.*

○ The **superlative** form is used to compare something or someone to two or more others:

> Das ist die **teuerste** Bluse.   *That is the most expensive blouse.*

Pronouns

○ A pronoun stands in for a noun to avoid repetition:

> **er** *he*   **uns** *us*

○ **Relative pronouns** are used to express *who* or *which:*

> Der Mann, **der** mit mir arbeitet, heißt Karl.
> *The man who works with me is called Karl.*

○ **Reflexive pronouns** refer back to the subject:

> Ich wasche **mich.**   *I wash myself.*

Cases

○ Case indicates the role of a noun or pronoun in the sentence. German has four cases: nominative, accusative, dative and genitive.

○ The **nominative** case is used for the subject of the sentence:

Der Mann heißt Karl.   *The man is called Karl.*

○ The **accusative** case differs from the nominative only for some pronouns and for masculine singular nouns. It is used to indicate the **direct object** of the action of the sentence:

Ich kenne **den Mann.**   *I know the man.*

○ The **dative** is used for the **indirect object**, the person to whom something is being given, shown etc.

Ich zeige **dem Mann** den Weg.   *I show (to) the man the way.*

○ The **genitive** is used to indicate possession:

die Freunde **des Mannes**   *the man's friends*
(the friends of the man)

○ The case of a noun or pronoun may also be determined by prepositions and some verbs.

Verbs

○ A verb is a word which tells us what someone or something does or is or what someone thinks or feels.

Susan **fährt** nach Deutschland.   *Susan goes to Germany.*

○ The above example is in the **present tense** because it indicates something going on at the time of speaking.

○ To talk about things that have happened in the past, German uses either the **simple past:**

Sie **lernte** Deutsch in der Schule.   *She learnt German at school.*

or the *perfect tense:*

Susan **hat** Deutsch **gelernt.**   *Susan has learnt German.*

or to describe events even further back, the *pluperfect tense:*

Sie **hatte** Deutsch **gelernt.**   *She had learnt German.*

○ In the above examples, the verb or the first part of the verb takes an ending which reflects the person or thing which is its subject. A verb form which takes such an ending is known as a *finite verb*. The perfect and pluperfect tenses are composed of a finite form of **haben** or **sein** together with the *past participle*.

○ German verbs are categorised as *strong verbs* or *weak verbs*. Weak verbs (of which **lernen** above is a good example) form their simple past with endings **-te, -test** etc. and their past participle ends in **-t**. Strong verbs form their simple past with no endings on the first and third person singular, and their past participle ends in -**n** (e.g. **singen**, simple past **ich sang**, perfect **ich habe gesungen**).

○ German also has a *present participle* which is often used as an adjective:

ein **singender** Polizist   *a singing policeman*

○ The most important non-finite form of a verb is the *infinitive*. This is the form listed in dictionaries and equates to the English *to:*

singen   *to sing*

○ To express actions in the *future*, German uses a finite form of **werden** together with the infinitive.

○ German has many *compound verbs* which may be *separable* or *inseparable*. With a separable verb, a prefix is added which remains joined to the verb in all non-finite forms but goes to the end of the clause in finite forms.

aufstehen   *to get up*
Ich **stehe** früh **auf.**   *I get up early.*

○ With an *inseparable verb*, the two parts always remain joined.

Ich **unterschreibe** den Brief.   *I sign the letter.*

○ Where the emphasis is on the action rather than on the subject, and especially if the subject is not stated, you use the *passive*. This consists of a finite form of **werden** together with the *past participle*.

> Die Briefe **werden sortiert.**   *Letters are sorted.*

○ German has two *subjunctive* forms, subjunctive 1 and subjunctive 2. Subjunctives are used respectively for what somebody else has said and to express what might happen:

> Er sagt, er **sei** Student.   *He says he is a student.*
> Wenn ich reich **wäre** ...   *If I were rich ...*

○ The *imperative* form is used for instructions and requests.

> **Gib** mir bitte den Flaschen-   *Please give me the bottle-*
> öffner.   *opener.*

Adverbs

○ An *adverb* is used to say more about a verb, an adjective or another adverb.

> Sie spricht **gut** Deutsch.   *She speaks German well.*
> Die Bluse ist **sehr** schön.   *The blouse is very nice.*

○ In German, adjectives can be used as adverbs without any further ending. In addition, there are some adverbs which can only be used as such, e.g. **sehr** (*very*), **beispielsweise** (*for example*).

○ A small number of adverbs also serve as *particles,* i.e. they carry no meaning but affect the tone of the sentence.

> Frag **doch mal** deine Mutter.   *Go on, ask your mother.*

Prepositions and conjunctions

○ A *preposition* is used to integrate a noun or pronoun into the rest of the sentence, normally in a phrase which indicates time, place or how an action is done. Prepositions determine the case of the following pronoun or noun.

durch das Fenster
mit dem Zug
um vier Uhr

through the window
by train
at four o'clock

- **Conjunctions** join together two words or two parts of a sentence.

Es wird gesungen **und** getanzt.

There was singing and dancing.

Einige geben auf, **weil** es zu schwer ist.

Some give up because it is too difficult.

The sentence

- A complete sentence must contain at least one finite verb. In a German **statement**, only one concept comes before the finite verb.

Große Unterschiede gibt es nicht.
There are no major differences.

- In a **question** or **request**, the verb can begin the sentence.

Kommt er aus Deutschland?
Singt uns ein Lied!

Does he come from Germany?
Sing us a song.

- A sentence will contain at least one **main clause**. There may be more than one main clause:

Carla kommt aus Deutschland, aber Susan kommt aus England.
Carla comes from Germany, but Susan comes from England.

- There may also be one or more **subordinate clauses**. In a German subordinate clause, the finite verb goes to the end.

Ich fahre nach Deutschland, weil ich Deutsch lernen **will.**
I am going to Germany because I want to learn German.

Saying who does what

Willst du mit ihr tanzen?

Woher kommt ihr?

Susan und Jane kommen aus Hertfordshire und besuchen ihre Brieffreundinnen Carla und Ute in Frankfurt. Aber sonst kennen sie **niemanden** in Deutschland. Die vier Mädchen **gehen** zusammen zur Disko des Sportvereins. Hans, ein Freund von Ute und Carla, stellt ihnen einige Fragen.   1.8 / 1.2

| Carla | Guten Tag, Hans. Ute und ich bringen heute unsere Brieffreundinnen aus England mit. **Sie** sind zu Besuch bei **uns**. **Wir** sind ja Mitglieder des Sportvereins. Können sie hier bleiben? | 1.1
1.7 / 1.1 |
| Hans | Aber klar. Woher **kommt ihr**? | 1.2 / 1.1 |

8

Susan	Ich **komme** aus Hatfield. Wissen Sie, wo Hatfield liegt?	1.2
Hans	Nein, das **weiß** ich nicht, aber das erklärst du **mir** bestimmt. Ich schlage überhaupt vor, dass wir uns duzen. Natürlich, wenn es **euch** recht ist. Ich duze Carla and Ute auch.	1.3 / 1.7 — 1.7
Susan	Ich denke, das **dauert** doch eine Weile …	1.2
Hans	Ach, was! Wir **sind** in Deutschland nicht mehr so förmlich und höflich, wie das in euren englischen Schulbüchern steht. Unter **uns** Sportlern ist das „Du" schon lange die Norm. Also, ich heiße Hans. Und wie heißt deine Freundin? Ich kenne **sie** noch nicht.	1.4 — 1.7 — 1.6
Susan	Entschuldigen Sie, eh, entschuldige, darf ich dir Jane vorstellen? **Sie kommt** auch aus der Nähe von Hatfield.	1.2
Hans	Guten Tag, Jane.	
Jane	Guten Tag, Hans. Vielen Dank, dass wir hier bleiben dürfen. Ich **bin** sehr froh, junge Leute in einer Disko kennen zu lernen, und dann noch in der Disko des Sportvereins. Können wir etwas für **dich** tun?	1.4 — 1.6
Hans	**Singt** uns doch bitte ein englisches Lied, damit wir etwas von England lernen. Jean-Marie kommt aus Paris, **er singt** dann noch einen französischen Chanson. **Tanzt du** mit **mir**? Peter, **komm** mal her, hier ist **jemand** aus England, willst du mit **ihr** tanzen? Sie heißt übrigens Susan.	1.5 — 1.1 / 1.2 — 1.3 / 1.5 — 1.8 / 1.7

1.1 Pronouns in the nominative

er singt	sie sind zu Besuch
woher kommt ihr?	wir sind Mitglieder

○ We use the term ***pronoun*** to mean a small word which stands in for the name of a person or thing. If we are talking about Susan, we may not wish to say *Susan* every time, but we could say *she*.

The term ***nominative*** distinguishes those pronouns which denote the subject of the sentence (*I, we, she*) from others such as *me, us, them* which we shall consider later in this chapter.

The nominative pronouns in German are:

	Singular		Plural	
1st person (the speaker)	**ich**	*I*	**wir**	*we*
2nd person (the person spoken to)	**du**	*you (familiar)*	**ihr**	*you (familiar)*
	Sie	*you (polite)*	**Sie**	*you (polite)*
3rd person (anybody or anything else)	**er**	*he* (or *it* for a masculine noun)	**sie**	*they*
	sie	*she* (or *it* for a feminine noun)		
	es	*it* (neuter noun)		

○ The choice of whether to use **du/ihr** or **Sie** can be problematic. For children, animals and close friends, **du** and **ihr** are used, while **Sie** is used for people you do not know. But among the younger generation, students etc. there is an increasing tendency to move to **du** fairly rapidly, as illustrated in the dialogue on page 9. In the plural it is possible to use **ihr** for a small group even if some of them are people to whom you would normally say **Sie**.

○ Note that **ich** is written with a lower case 'i' (unless, of course, it starts the sentence). Conversely, **Sie**, the formal *you* is always written with a capital.

A⟩⟩ Rewrite the following statements, replacing the words in italics with the appropriate pronoun.

1 *Hans* bittet Jane um einen Tanz.
2 *Jane* besucht ihre Freundin in Frankfurt.
3 *Susan, Jane, Carla und Ute* gehen zur Disko des Sportvereins.

B⟩⟩ Complete the following with the appropriate pronoun.

1 Carlas Eltern sagen: „___ fahren zusammen nach Alzey."
2 Susan fragt Jane: „Kommst ___ mit zur Disko des Sportvereins?"
3 Carla sagt zu ihren Eltern: „___ gehe heute abend mit Jane aus."
4 Carlas Mutter fragt die zwei Mädchen: „Wann kommt ___ heute abend zurück?"
5 Carla fragt ihren Lehrer: „Haben ___ Jane schon kennen gelernt?"

1.2 Present tense – regular

ich komme	sie kommt
die Mädchen gehen	er singt
das dauert	Woher kommt ihr?

● Verb forms in German consist mainly of a **stem** and an **ending**. The 'stem' is identified by taking the infinitive form (the form you can look up in a dictionary) and removing the final **-en** or **-n**. The 'ending' on the verb has to relate to the person doing the action; thus it is **ich singe** but **er singt** etc. The full list for **singen** (to sing) is:

ich	sing **e**
du	sing **st**
er/sie/es	sing **t**
wir/Sie/sie	sing **en**
ihr	sing **t**

Note that the 'infinitive' (the 'to ...' form which is the one you will find in dictionaries) always ends in **-n**. This is always the same as the **wir/Sie/sie** form (except in the case of **sein** – see section 1.4).

○ The vast majority of verbs in German follow this pattern. Further examples in this chapter are:

> bleiben — *to stay*
> kommen — *to come*
> besuchen — *to visit*

○ Don't fall into the trap of translating a phrase like *he is singing* with anything that starts **er ist ...**! While English has three ways of expresssing the present (e.g. *he sings, he is singing* and in questions *does he sing?*), German only has **er singt** and **singt er?**

A》 Study the following description of Carla's daily routine, and underline or make a note of all the verbs:

„Ich gehe jeden Tag zu Fuß zur Schule. Die Schule ist nicht weit vom Haus. Die erste Stunde beginnt um 7.50 Uhr. Meist komme ich sogar pünktlich! Mittags um 13.00 Uhr ist die Schule zu Ende. Nachmittags mache ich Schulaufgaben. Das geht sehr schnell. Meist besuche ich etwas später eine Freundin. Wir sitzen zusammen, plaudern, hören Musik, erzählen von Freunden und planen etwas für das Wochenende. Abends bleibe ich meistens zu Hause, aber manchmal gehe ich aus. Ganz selten spüle ich das Geschirr oder schreibe Briefe."

B》 Imagine that it is Ute who is describing Carla's daily routine. Write out how she would tell it. You will need to alter some of the verbs, but not all. Start: 'Sie geht jeden Tag ...'

C》 Susan takes a little while to get used to using 'du'. Here are some questions she asks Peter as they are dancing. How should she have phrased them?

1 Wo wohnen Sie?
2 Gehen Sie noch zur Schule?
3 Kommen Sie oft in die Disko?
4 Wie lange kennen Sie schon Carla?

1.3 Present tense – variations

> Tanzt du mit mir?   Das weiß ich nicht.

○ There are a number of verbs where the 2nd and 3rd person singular
(i.e. the **du** and the **er/sie/es** forms) are slightly different from
what they would be if the verb were completely regular.

Verbs whose stem ends in **-d** or **-t** add an additional **e** to make the
forms more pronounceable.

arbeiten (*to work*)	ich arbeite	du arbeit**est**	er arbeit**et**
finden (*to find*)	ich finde	du find**est**	er find**et**

Verbs ending in **-s**, **-ß**, **-ss** or **-z** do not add a further **s** in the 2nd
person.

tanzen (*to dance*)	ich tanze	du tan**zt**	er tanzt
heißen (*to be called*)	ich heiße	du hei**ßt**	er heißt

Many verbs whose stem vowel is **-e** change this in the 2nd and 3rd
persons to **i** or **ie.**

geben (*to give*)	ich gebe	du g**i**bst	er g**i**bt
sehen (*to see*)	ich sehe	du s**ie**hst	er s**ie**ht

Many verbs whose stem vowel is **a** or **au** add an umlaut in the 2nd
and 3rd person.

fahren (*to drive*)	ich fahre	du f**ä**hrst	er f**ä**hrt
laufen (*to run*)	ich laufe	du l**äu**fst	er l**äu**ft

The most important divergence in the 1st person (the **ich** form) is
with verbs ending in **-eln**. Here the **e** is often dropped.

basteln (*to build*)	ich bast**le**	du bastelst	er bastelt
sammeln (*to collect*)	ich samm**le**	du sammelst	er sammelt

○ A verb which is irregular in the whole of the singular is:

wissen (*to know*)	ich weiß	du weißt	er weiß

○ In a good dictionary, you will find these words listed in a list of 'German irregular verbs' (sometimes 'German strong verbs'). Some of the most important verbs are listed on pages 112-113 of this book.

A》 Write out the full present tense of:

1 lesen
2 fahren
3 arbeiten

B》 In the course of the dance, Susan tells Peter about herself. Later he relates to Hans what he has found out about her. Here are Susan's statements; how does Peter relate them?

e.g. Ich lese jeden Morgen die Zeitung.
Sie liest jeden Morgen die Zeitung.

1 Ich fahre gern zum Einkaufen in die Großstadt.
2 Ich bastle gern Geschenke für die Familie.
3 Ich sammle Briefmarken.
4 Ich arbeite samstags als Verkäuferin in einem Gemüsegeschäft.
5 Ich schreibe gern Briefe.

C》 Susan writes to her friend in England what Peter has told her. Here is Peter's story; retell it as she would, beginning with 'Er kommt ...'

Ich komme aus Usingen und arbeite als Computerprogrammierer in Frankfurt. Ich spreche etwas Englisch, in der Computerindustrie sprechen wir fast alle Englisch. Ich finde die Arbeit sehr interessant. Ich treibe viel Sport, besonders Leichtathletik und laufe 100 m.

Ich bastle gern Geschenke für die Familie

1.4 *Sein* and *haben*

Ich bin sehr froh	Wir sind nicht mehr so förmlich.

○ 'To be' and 'to have' are irregular in most languages. In German the forms are:

	sein	haben
	to be	*to have*
ich	bin	habe
du	bist	hast
er/sie/es	ist	hat
wir/Sie/sie	sind	haben
ihr	seid	habt

○ Note that **sein** is the only verb in German where the **wir/Sie/sie** form is different from the infinitive.

A》 Complete the following with the appropriate form of 'sein':

1 Ich ___ Deutsche.
2 Sie ___ Polin.
3 Das ist Jean Paul. Er ___ Franzose.
4 Du ___ Engländerin.
5 Wir ___ alle Europäer!
6 Ihr ___ Ausländer, nicht wahr?
7 Die Mädchen kenne ich nicht. ___ sie aus England?
8 Ich habe ein Haustier. Es ___ ein Kätzchen.

B》 Insert the appropriate form of 'haben':

1 Ich ___ einen Bruder, der im Tennis viele Pokale gewinnt.
2 ___ du eine Schwester? Hans ___ eine Schwester, die in Alzey ein Weingut ___.
3 Das Kätzchen ___ ein schmutziges Wollbällchen.
4 Wir ___ an unserer Schule zur Zeit viele Engländer und Franzosen zu Besuch. Sie ___ alle sehr gute Deutschkenntnisse. ___ ihr auch oft Schüler aus anderen europäischen Ländern zu Besuch?
5 Carla fragt ihren Trainer: „___ Sie etwas dagegen, wenn ich meine englische Freundin zum Training mitbringe?"

1.5 Imperatives

> Komm mal her!   Singt uns ein Lied!

○ The term **imperative** strictly speaking means *command*, but these forms are used for polite requests as well. Their formation is simple.

○ If you are addressing someone as **du**, the imperative form is the same as the **ich** form, with the final **-e** usually dropped.

		Imperative
kommen (*to come*)	ich komme	komm!
fahren (*to drive*)	ich fahre	fahr!

e.g. Komm bitte morgen wieder!
Please come again tomorrow.

But verbs which change the **e** vowel to **i** or **ie** in the 2nd person also change it in the imperative.

e.g.	geben (*to give*)	du gibst	gib!
	sehen (*to see*)	du siehst	sieh!

sein has an irregular form:

sein		ich bin, du bist	sei!

○ For groups of people whom you address as **ihr**, the imperative stays the same. There are no exceptions.

kommen	ihr kommt	kommt!
fahren	ihr fahrt	fahrt!
sein	ihr seid	seid!

○ For people whom you address as **Sie**, the imperative is again the same form, but the verb precedes the pronoun.

kommen	Sie kommen	kommen Sie!
fahren	Sie fahren	fahren Sie!

The only exception is **sein**:

sein   Sie sind   seien Sie!

NOTE There is traditionally (but not always in modern German) an exclamation mark at the end of the sentence in which an imperative is used.

>> Complete the following requests using the verbs in brackets:

1   Peter, ___ mir bitte deine Adresse!   (geben)
2   Peter, ___ mal her!   (kommen)
3   Peter, ___ mit Susan!   (tanzen)
4   Kinder, ___ bitte für mich zum Supermarkt!   (gehen)
5   Susan und Jane, ___ uns doch bitte ein   (singen)
     englisches Lied!
6   ___ mir bitte sofort, wenn du in Deutschland bist!   (schreiben)
7   ___ Sie diese Tabletten dreimal täglich!   (nehmen)
8   ___ Sie mir bitte, wo Cambridge liegt!   (sagen)
9   ___ drei Eier und ___ sie in die Pfanne, dann   (holen, schlagen)
     hast du schnell etwas zu essen.

1.6 Pronouns in the accusative

für dich   Ich kenne sie noch nicht.

○   Compare the following sentences in English.

> *He is in the room.*   *I can see him.*

The reason we use *he* in the first example and *him* in the second is that in the first sentence, *he* is the subject of the sentence, i.e. he is doing the action, whereas in the second sentence, *he* is on the receiving end of the action, i.e. is the 'object'. Similar pairs in English are *I—me, we—us, they—them* etc.

The grammatical term for these object forms is ***the accusative case***. The accusative forms of the pronouns are as follows. You will note that not all of them differ from the nominative.

	Singular		Plural	
	Nom.	Acc.	Nom.	Acc.
1st person	ich	**mich**	wir	**uns**
2nd person	du	**dich**	ihr	**euch**
	Sie	Sie	Sie	Sie
3rd person	er	**ihn**	sie	sie
	sie	sie		
	es	es		

○ Remember that **es** can only stand in place of a neuter noun; masculine and feminine nouns in the accusative are replaced by **ihn** and **sie** respectively.

○ The accusative is also used after certain prepositions (short words which indicate relationships, e.g. *for, without*). The most important of these are:

durch	*through*	**ohne**	*without*
für	*for*	**um**	*around*
gegen	*against*		

≫ Answer the following questions with 'Ja, …' and shorten your replies by replacing the words in italics with the appropriate pronoun.

e.g. Kaufst du *die neue Schallplatte*?
Ja, ich kaufe sie.

1 Kennst du *Peter*?
2 Kennst du *Jane*?
3 Besuchst du *meine Eltern* nächste Woche?
4 Schickst du *das Paket* nach England?
5 Liest du *die Zeitung*?
6 Schreibst du *den Brief*?
7 Hast du einen Brief für *Carla*?
8 Hast du ein Geschenk für *Hans*?
9 Schreibst du *den Brief* morgen?
10 Verstehst du *mich*?
11 Siehst du *uns*?

1.7 Pronouns in the dative

zu Besuch bei uns	unter uns
wenn es euch recht ist	Willst du mit ihr tanzen?
das erklärst du mir	Tanzt du mit mir?

○ There is a third form of the pronouns, known as the ***dative case***. This is used primarily to indicate the person to whom something is given, shown, told etc.

e.g. Ich gebe **ihr** Blumen.
*I give **her** flowers (I give the flowers **to her**).*

Here the object of the action is clearly the flowers. We could in English say *to her*, but we would not always do so. To express the *to ...* idea, German uses the dative.

○ The forms of the dative in German are:

	Singular			Plural		
	Nom.	Acc.	Dat.	Nom.	Acc.	Dat.
1	ich	mich	**mir**	wir	uns	uns
2	du	dich	**dir**	ihr	euch	euch
	Sie	Sie	**Ihnen**	Sie	Sie	**Ihnen**
3	er	ihn	**ihm**	sie	sie	**ihnen**
	sie	sie	**ihr**			
	es	es	**ihm**			

○ The most important verbs which frequently require both an accusative and a dative object are:

geben *to give*   **schenken** *to give as a present*
zeigen *to show*   **erklären** *to explain*

e.g. Ich gebe **ihr** den Schlüssel.
I give her the key.

O There are also some verbs which require a dative as their only object. They are normally verbs which indicate some sort of indirect effect, e.g. **helfen** *to help*, which can be expressed as *to give help to*, or **danken** *to thank* = *to give thanks to*.

The main verbs with dative objects are:

danken	*to thank*	**gehören**	*to belong to*
erzählen	*to tell*	**helfen**	*to help*
folgen	*to follow*		

e.g. Ich helfe **ihm**.
I help (= give help to) him.

Das Buch gehört **mir**.
The book belongs to me.

O In addition, there are some very frequent stock phrases which involve datives. These include:

Es gefällt mir.	*I like it.*
Wie geht es dir/Ihnen?	*How are you?*
Es tut mir Leid.	*I am sorry.*
Mir ist warm.	*I am feeling warm.*
Was fehlt dir?	*What's wrong with you?*
Das ist mir recht.	*That's all right by me.*

O The most frequent prepositions taking the dative are:

aus	*from*	**seit**	*since*
bei	*at, at the home of*	**von**	*from*
mit	*with*	**zu**	*to*
nach	*after, to*		

e.g. **Sie sind zu Besuch bei mir.**
They are visiting (and staying with) me.

Sie geht mit ihr in die Disko.
She goes with her to the disco.

A⟩⟩ In the following statements about Jane's stay at Carla's home, replace the words in italics with the appropriate pronoun.

e.g. Jane und Susan helfen *Carlas Mutter*.
Jane und Susan helfen ihr.

1   Jane wohnt bei *Carla*.
2   Das Haus gehört *Carlas Eltern*.
3   Carla zeigt *Jane* die Sehenswürdigkeiten von Frankfurt.
4   Jane fährt auch mit *Carla* nach Heidelberg.
5   Jane erzählt *Carlas Bruder* von ihrer Schule in England.
6   Jane gibt *Carlas Eltern* ein Geschenk aus England.
7   Carlas Eltern danken *Jane* dafür.

B⟩⟩ Carla's mother also asks Jane a lot of questions. Answer them on Jane's behalf, remembering to be as polite and helpful as possible to your German hostess! She may use 'du' to you, but you reply with 'Sie'.

1   Hilfst du uns im Hause?
2   Sprichst du bitte etwas Englisch mir mir?
3   Geht es dir gut?
4   Wohnst du gerne bei uns?
5   Gefällt es dir hier in Frankfurt?
6   Schreibst du uns aus England?

C⟩⟩ In the following sentences, some of the names in italics will need to be replaced with nominatives, some with accusatives and some with datives.

1   *Carla* wohnt in Frankfurt.
2   Wo ist *Peter*?
3   Carla schenkt *Susan* ein Buch über Frankfurt.
4   Peter kennt *Susan* noch nicht.
5   Susan kennt *Peter* auch noch nicht.
6   Susan erzählt *Carla und Ute* von England.
7   *Peter* tanzt mit *Jane*.
8   Susan zeigt *Peter* einige Bilder von ihrer Familie.
9   Frankfurt gefällt *Susan* gut.
10   Das ist ein Bild von *Susans Mutter*.

1.8 Saying *anybody* and *nobody*

sie kennen niemanden   hier ist jemand

○ The German equivalent for *somebody* is **jemand**, and for *nobody*, **niemand**.

e.g. **Hier ist jemand aus England.**
Here is someone from England.

Hier ist niemand.
There is nobody here.

The case forms are:

Nominative	**jemand**	**niemand**
Accusative	**jemand(en)**	**niemand(en)**
Dative	**jemand(em)**	**niemand(em)**

○ As you see, you can use them in the accusative and dative with or without an ending. In modern spoken and written German, the forms without ending are more common.

e.g. **Peter spricht mit jemandem.**
Peter spricht mit jemand.
Peter is talking to someone.

Ich kenne hier niemanden.
Ich kenne hier niemand.
I know nobody (around) here.

○ To say *someone else* or *nobody else*, use **jemand anders** and **niemand anders.**

e.g. **Niemand anders war da.**
Nobody else was there.

A vague *somebody or other* is **irgendjemand.**
e.g. **Peter spricht mit irgendjemandem.**
Peter spricht mit irgendjemand.
Peter is talking to someone or other.

○ In questions and negatives, **jemand** corresponds to the English *anybody*.

e.g. **Ist da jemand?**
Is anyone there?

Ist da irgendjemand?
Is anyone at all there?

Ich bin nicht irgendjemand.
I'm not just anybody.

A⟩⟩ Complete the following sentences by translating the words in italics.

e.g. Ich kenne (*nobody*) in Frankfurt.
Ich kenne niemanden in Frankfurt.
OR Ich kenne niemand in Frankfurt.

1 Kennen Sie (*anybody*) in London?
2 Hier ist (*nobody*) außer mir.
3 Hans schreibt (*to somebody*) in Hatfield.
4 Die Aufgaben sind schwer und (*nobody*) will mir helfen.
5 (*Nobody*) geht ans Telefon, aber (*somebody*) muss da sein.
6 Ist (*anybody*) in der Küche? Ich möchte eine Tasse Tee.
7 (*Nobody*) anders kann so schnell laufen.
8 Gehört dieses Buch (*to anybody*)?
9 Ich bin nicht (*just anybody*). Ich bin doch die Johanna.

B⟩⟩ Once again translate the words in italics, this time to practise several points you have learnt in this chapter.

Susan (*comes from*) Hatfield in der Nähe von London. (*She goes*) auf eine Mädchenschule und (*she likes it*). (*She is learning*) vier Fächer: Deutsch, Geschichte, Erdkunde und Englisch. (*She finds*) Geschichte ganz leicht, aber Deutsch (*is*) sehr schwer. Sie treibt viel Sport, besonders Leichtathletik. (*She runs*) gern 100 m. Samstags (*she goes*) oft mit ihren Freundinnen in die Disko, aber manchmal (*they go*) auch nach London. (*She is going*) jetzt nach Frankfurt, aber (*she knows nobody*) in Deutschland außer Carla.

2 | Talking about people and things

Beim Ernten helfen alle mit

Auf dem Weingut

Hans fährt Carla und Susan nach Alzey; sie besuchen den **Schwager** und die **Schwägerin** von Hans, die dort ein **Weingut** haben.		2.2 2.3

Hans	Susan, das ist mein Schwager Karl. Er ist der Winzer in unserer Familie.	
Susan	Guten Tag, Herr Höfer. Hans hat mir schon von Ihnen erzählt. Das ist das erste **Mal**, dass ich auf einem Weingut bin.	2.1 / 2.2
Karl	Herzlich willkommen! Was kann ich Ihnen über unsere **Weine** erzählen?	2.4
Susan	Ist das ein Familienbetrieb?	
Karl	Ja, fast alle **Weingüter** hier sind immer noch **Familienbetriebe**. Aber wir arbeiten als Winzergenossenschaft zusammen und verkaufen unsere Weine in alle Welt.	2.3 / 2.4 2.3 / 2.4

Susan	Arbeiten nur die **Familienmitglieder** bei der Weinlese?	2.3/2.4
Karl	Ja, das machen wir alles selbst.	
Elfriede	Was erzählt Ihnen mein Mann jetzt? **Der** spinnt wirklich. Bei der Weinlese brauchen wir **jedes Jahr** viele **Helfer**. **Dieses Jahr** waren auch junge Leute aus Osteuropa da, ein **polnischer Student** und seine **ungarische Freundin**. **Die** wollen auch nächstes Jahr wiederkommen. Beim **Ernten** helfen alle mit.	2.6 2.7 2.4 / 2.7 2.1 2.1 / 2.6 2.1 / 2.2
Karl	Aber die Familienmitglieder müssen eben doch sehr viel machen. Unsere Tochter ist **Studentin**, aber sie hat Gott sei Dank im **September** noch **Semesterferien**, da hilft sie auch mit.	2.5 2.1 / 2.2 2.3 / 2.5
Elfriede	Als **Winzerstochter** muss sie das!	2.3 / 2.5
Susan	**Welche Weine** haben Sie vorwiegend? Sind es nur **Weißweine**?	2.7 2.3
Karl	Also, die Pfalz ist eigentlich durch ihre Weißweine bekannt. Aber in Deutschland gibt es auch sehr gute **Rotweine**. Die müssen Sie auch probieren!	2.3

2.1 Capital letters for nouns

| das erste Mal | beim Ernten | im September |
| ein polnischer Student | seine ungarische Freundin | |

○ We use the term *noun* to denote the name of a person, place, thing or concept. In writing German, we need to know which are the nouns, because they are written with a capital letter:

e.g. **der Schwager** **die Studentin** etc.

○ The most difficult nouns to identify are abstract nouns or nouns which derive from other forms of speech. For example, in the phrase *the first time*, the word *time* is a noun. So it is capitalised: **das erste Mal.** Similarly, although **ernten** *(to harvest)* would not take a capital, the noun **das Ernten** *(harvesting)* does.

○ Note particularly that in German, it is only the nouns which are capitalised. Adjectives are never capitalised even if they refer to names of countries, etc. Compare the English and German:

ein polnischer Student *a Polish student*

The only occasion when words such as *Polish* or *German* are written with a capital is when referring to the language or school subject, or when they form part of a unique name:

Wir lernen Deutsch. *We are learning German.*
die Französische Revolution *the French Revolution*

Only adjectives from town names are always capitalised:

der Kölner Karneval *Cologne Carnival*

○ As in English, any word beginning a sentence starts with a capital.

》 Rewrite the following putting capital letters where required:

1 der wein ist sehr herb.
2 meine arbeit ist abwechslungsreich.
3 die stimmung bei der weinlese ist sehr kameradschaftlich.
4 viele leute in der welt lernen englisch.
5 eine englische studentin und ihr deutscher freund lernen zusammen spanisch. das lernen macht ihnen spaß.

...

2.2 Gender

der Schwager	die Schwägerin	das Weingut
der September	das Mal	das Ernten

○ All nouns in German belong to one of three *genders*. The gender of the noun is reflected in the *definite article (the)*, i.e.

> singular masculine nouns are preceded by **der**
> singular neuter nouns are preceded by **das**
> singular feminine nouns are preceded by **die**.

○ In some cases, the gender of a noun will be fairly obvious from its meaning. Thus most nouns referring to male persons are masculine, most referring to female persons are feminine, etc. But even here there are exceptions, notably **das Mädchen** and **das Fräulein** (because all nouns ending in -**chen** and -**lein** are neuter; see page 28). The problem comes with nouns which have no obvious gender. Apart from a few general rules listed below, the only safe guideline is to learn each noun's gender as you go along. Dictionaries help the learner by indicating **der, das** or **die** for each noun or give an indication of gender by an abbreviation, such as:

> *m*   for masculine
> *nt* for neuter (to avoid confusion with *n*, which can simply indicate *noun)*
> *f*   for feminine

○ The following general guidelines may be helpful:

Masculine nouns include:

a) Names of the days, months and seasons
   der Montag; der September; der Frühling

b) Makes of cars (because it's **der Wagen**)
   der BMW; der Opel

c) Nouns ending in **-ant, -ich, -ig, -ing, -ismus, -ist, -or**
   der Passant; der Teppich; der Honig; der Motor
   (exception: **das Labor**)

Neuter nouns include:

a)   nouns indicating 'little' and ending in **-chen or -lein:**
     das Mädchen, das Fräulein

b)   names of hotels, restaurants and cinemas:
     das Hilton, das Kranzler, das Roxy

c)   other parts of speech (e.g. verbs) used as nouns:
     das Ernten, das Lernen

Feminine nouns include:

a)   Most names of rivers:
     die Elbe; die Ruhr; die Themse
     (but important exceptions include **der Rhein, der Main**
     and **der Neckar**!)

b)   Names of motorbikes, aeroplanes and ships:
     die BMW; die Boeing; die Bremen

c)   nouns ending in **-heit, -keit, -ei, -ie, -ion, -schaft, -ung**
     die Einheit, die Biologie, die Bedeutung

◉ Many of the words denoting nationality and profession have both
   masculine and feminine forms, as do the names of animals:

der Engländer	**die Engländerin**
der Lehrer	**die Lehrerin**
der Bauer	**die Bäuerin**
der Kater	**die Katze**

A» Use the rules on pages 27-28 to determine the gender of the
following:
1   Mercedes
2   Bedienung
3   Schönheit
4   Nation
5   Käfig
6   Gesellschaft
7   Idealismus
8   Skilaufen
9   Märchen
10   Mittwoch

B》 Elfriede tells Susan more about her life in the vineyard:

Die Arbeit hier ist sehr abwechslungsreich. Ich möchte nicht in der Stadt wohnen. Ich spreche mit den Kunden (wir verkaufen hier im Ausschank Wein), mache meine Abrechnung für das Finanzamt, bestelle die Helfer für die Weinlese und was so alles anfällt. Oft organisiere ich auch Weinproben für den Verkehrsverein. Ich treffe viele Besucher aus aller Welt, erzähle etwas über die verschiedenen Reben und über die Qualität des Weines. Das interessiert sie immer. Natürlich trinken wir den Wein aus unseren Alzeyer Weingläsern. Die dürfen die Besucher dann mit nach Hause nehmen.

From the above passage, pick out all the nouns and list them with their genders. You may need to look up most of them in a dictionary (unless, of course, you know or can work out their genders).

C》 There are a few pairs of words in German where the same word is used with different genders to indicate quite different meanings. Look up the following in your dictionary and list both genders and both meanings for each:

1 Gehalt
2 Kunde
3 Leiter
4 Flur
5 Golf
6 See

2.3 Compound nouns

der Weißwein	der Rotwein	die Familienmitglieder
der Familienbetrieb	das Weingut	die Semesterferien
die Winzerstochter		

○ Many nouns in German are composed of two or more parts. This is a feature of German which is far less common in other languages, and which can be used for efficiency of language.

e.g. **Familienmitglieder**
members of the family

○ Some compounds, however, require the insertion of a linking element such as **-s-** or **-n-** between two of the components.

e.g. **die Winzerstochter**
der Familienbetrieb

○ In all compound nouns it is the final component which indicates the essence of the item being described; all preceding components serve to give additional information. Thus a **Familienbetrieb** is a type of **Betrieb.** A **Rotwein** is a type of wine, etc.

It is also the final component which determines the gender of the compound:

die Familie + der Betrieb = der Familienbetrieb
der Wein + das Gut = das Weingut

○ But be careful with the meaning of compounds. They do not always mean only the sum of the two meanings! For example, **das Haus** is *the house* and **der Meister** is *the master* but **der Hausmeister** is *the caretaker*! A good dictionary has to decide which compounds to list of the very many possible ones, and will try to include those whose meaning cannot be worked out from the individual parts!

A〉〉 Form compound nouns from the following pairs of components. Give the meaning and gender for each compound.

1	der Rat	das Haus
2	der Punkt	die Zeit
3	der Betrieb	die Familie
4	der Schein	der Führer
5	das Buch	das Wort
6	die Küche	der Schrank
7	die Industrie	das Automobil

B〉〉 Look up the following in the dictionary and decide whether the meaning of the compound is more than the sum of the parts.

1	das Einhorn	5	die Erdbeere
2	der Wasserstoff	6	der Kofferraum
3	das Damenfahrrad	7	das Frostschutzmittel
4	das Parkhaus	8	der Gartenzwerg

2.4 Plurals

Weingüter	Familienbetriebe	viele Helfer
unsere Weine	Familienmitglieder	

○ In English, it is generally easy to form the plural of nouns; you simply add '-s'. *The girl* becomes *the girls*, *the dog* becomes *the dogs* etc. But there are exceptions such as *men, mice, sheep,* etc.

In German, there are several ways of forming plurals. As with genders, the only safe rule is to learn them as you go along.

In a dictionary, you will normally find two endings given after each noun. The first of these is usually the genitive (possessive) which will be covered in Unit 3. The second ending is the plural one, and the one which concerns us here. For example, for **der Betrieb** you would find the endings given as **-s/-e**. This means that the genitive form ends in an **-s**, the plural in an **-e**: **Betriebe.** Sometimes, the ending is shown as **¨e** or **¨er**. This means that besides adding the **-e** or **-er**, you also need to add an umlaut to the stressed vowel in the word itself. Thus **das Weingut, -s / ¨er** means that the plural is **Weingüter.**

○ Despite the general rule about learning plurals as you go along, there are a number of categories of plural which it is helpful to know.

Masculine
The most common plural is **-e**, usually with umlaut if there is a vowel (a, o or u) which can take one.

der Wein	die Weine
der Gast	die Gäste

But there are a number of nouns which could take umlaut but do not:

der Tag	die Tage

Masculines ending in **-el, -er, -en** usually add nothing to form the plural, but they may take an umlaut.

der Helfer	die Helfer
der Mantel	die Mäntel

Neuter
Many common neuter nouns add **-e** (no umlaut):

    das Spiel   **die Spiele**

while others add **-er**, with umlaut if possible:

    das Haus   **die Häuser**

Feminine
Feminines usually add **-n** or **-en** if appropriate to make the plural more easily pronounceable:

    die Lampe   **die Lampen**
    die Wohnung   **die Wohnungen**

but there are several common feminines which add **-e** and an umlaut:

    die Stadt   **die Städte**

Feminines with **-in** double the **n** before adding **-en**:

    die Lehrerin   **die Lehrerinnen**

Imported words
Some words imported from other languages have also imported an **-s** plural:

    das Appartement   **die Appartements**

○   The easy aspect of plurals in German is that the definite article in the nominative case is always **die**.

A» Rewrite the following sentences so that they refer to the plural. Note that you will need to alter not only the nouns and articles *(the)* but also the verbs (see Unit 1).

1   Die Studentin studiert in Heidelberg.
2   Der Winzer arbeitet sehr viel.
3   Die Winzerstochter hilft immer mit.
4   Das Weingut liegt bei Alzey.
5   Das Weinglas ist kaputt.
6   Das Auto fährt sehr schnell.
7   Der Kunde probiert den Rotwein.

B» A small number of nouns have two meanings with separate plurals. Look up the meanings of:

1 die Mütter - die Muttern
2 die Banken - die Bänke
3 die Strauße - die Sträuße
4 die Hähne - die Hahnen

2.5 Omission of the article

> unsere Tochter ist Studentin   als Winzerstochter
>
> sie hat Semesterferien

○ In general, the article is used in German much as in English, i.e. where English requires an article, so does German. But there are some instances where English uses an article but German does not.

In particular, this applies to somebody's job, nationality or faith.

Er ist Ungar.   *He is a Hungarian.*
Sie ist Studentin.   *She is a student.*
Sie ist Katholikin.   *She is a Catholic.*

○ German frequently omits the article where English might use *some* or *any*.

Ich möchte Rotwein.   *I would like some red wine.*
Haben Sie Weißwein?   *Do you have any white wine?*

» In the following examples, say what each of the people concerned does for a living. Remember that some may need feminine forms!

e.g. Monika studiert in Frankfurt.
       Sie ist Studentin

1 Hans dient in der Armee.
2 Herr Höfer baut Wein an.
3 Herr Grimm predigt in der Kirche.
4 Susan geht noch zur Schule.
5 Herr Wilhelm bäckt Brot.
6 Frau Meier unterrichtet Deutsch.

2.6 Articles as pronouns

der spinnt   die wollen wiederkommen

- The definite article can also be used as a pronoun. It is preferred to the 3rd person pronoun in colloquial language and to give emphasis, since the pronoun cannot normally take the stress in a sentence.

  e. g. Der Lehrer hat lange Ferien. **Der** hat es gut!
  Monika studiert acht Stunden pro Tag. **Die** ist fleißig!

>> Rewrite the following sentences, emphasising the pronoun by replacing it with the appropriate article.

1   Kennen Sie Susan? Sie wohnt in Hertfordshire.
2   Der Wein ist sieben Jahre alt. Er ist teuer.
3   Susan tanzt mit Peter. Er kann gut tanzen.
4   Das Haus ist nicht weit vom Weingut. Es liegt schön.
5   Es gibt nur wenige deutsche Rotweine, aber sie schmecken sehr gut.

Monika studiert acht Stunden pro Tag. Die ist fleißig!

2.7 Saying *this, every* and *which*?

jedes Jahr	dieses Jahr	welche Weine

○ The following words take similar endings to the definite article

Masculine	Neuter	Feminine and Plural	
dieser	**dieses**	**diese**	*this*
jeder	**jedes**	**jede** (no plural)	*every*
jener	**jenes**	**jene**	*that*
welcher	**welches**	**welche**	*which*

e.g. **dieser Wein** *this wine*
jede Woche *every week*
welche Weine? *which wines?*

○ In spoken German, **jener** is used far less often than in written German.

≫ Write out the following sentences, translating into German the English word in italics.

1 *(This)* Wein schmeckt sehr gut.
2 *(Every)* Winzerstochter muss bei der Weinlese mithelfen.
3 *(Which)* Weine möchten Sie probieren?
4 *(This)* Weingut ist ein Familienbetrieb.
5 *(Every)* Weingut braucht viele Helfer.
6 *(Which)* Kunde kommt morgen?

3 Saying who things belong to

Ich kann den Flaschenöffner nicht finden!

Ankunft am Campingplatz

Nach dem Besuch in Alzey gehen die jungen Leute zelten.
In der Nähe von Alzey ist **ein** schöner Zeltplatz. Natürlich   3.1
treffen sie dort noch mehr Leute.

Camper   Hallo! Ich heiße Rüdiger. Sind das **eure** Sachen?   3.2
            Woher kommt ihr?

Susan   Ich bin aus England. Aber **meine** Freundin ist aus   3.2
            Usingen. Und das sind nicht **unsere** Sachen!   3.2

36

Rüdiger	Du kommst aus England! Ach, ich habe Verwandte in England! Aber wo genau? Ja, ich weiß es. **Ein** 3.1 **Onkel** wohnt in Manchester, der ist dort Ingenieur. Ich wusste sogar den **Namen seiner** Firma, aber 3.6 / 3.5 jetzt habe ich ihn wieder vergessen.
Susan	Und du? Woher kommst du?
Rüdiger	Ursprünglich aus der Schweiz. Eine Branche **meiner** Familie ist immer noch in der Schweiz. 3.5
Susan	Sehr interessant, deine Familie! Aber ich habe nach dir selbst gefragt. Wo wohnst du, zum Beispiel?
Rüdiger	Ach, meine Freunde fahren gerade weg, die warten nicht auf mich. Bis später!
Susan	Das ist aber ein komischer Typ! Er redet immer von **seiner** Familie! Reden deine Landsleute immer 3.4 so von **ihren** Familien? 3.4
Carla	Gott sei Dank nicht! Susan, hast du **unseren** 3.3 Flaschenöffner gesehen? Ich kann ihn nicht finden.
Susan	Bei **deinen** Klamotten, vielleicht? Das ist so 3.4 unordentlich hier.
Carla	Unordentlich? Ich sehe **keine** Unordnung! Aber du 3.1 hast Recht, hier ist **unser** Flaschenöffner! 3.2
Susan	Na, gut. Hast du nicht gesagt, dass du Peter und Hans zum Abendessen eingeladen hast?
Carla	Ja, sie werden wohl bald kommen. Wir müssen uns beeilen. Und hast du gehört? Im nächsten Zelt gibt es **einen Sachsen**! Man erkennt ihn sofort an 3.3 / 3.6 der Stimme! Den müssen wir auch kennen lernen.

3.1 Indefinite article and *kein*

ein Zeltplatz   keine Unordnung
Ein Onkel wohnt in Manchester.

○ The German *indefinite article* (meaning 'a') is **ein**. Its forms are:

masculine	**ein**	**ein Mann**
neuter	**ein**	**ein Haus**
feminine	**eine**	**eine Frau**

In these nominative forms, only the feminine form has an ending. Neither the masculine nor the neuter forms show the gender in the ending. We can say that they have no ending.

Examples from the dialogue:

In der Nähe von Alzey ist **ein** Zeltplatz.
*Near Alzey is **a** campsite.*

Ein Onkel wohnt in Manchester.
***An** uncle lives in Manchester.*

○ As in English, there is no plural form of **ein**. The article is omitted:

Heute Abend gibt es Bohnen.
Tonight we are having beans.

○ German also has a negative indefinite article, **kein.** This is used to express *not a* or *no* in such expressions as:

Ich habe kein Auto. *I don't have a car.*
Ich sehe keine Unordnung. *I can't see any untidiness.*

The forms of **kein** are similar to **ein**, i.e.

masculine	**kein**
neuter	**kein**
feminine	**keine**

and there is also a plural form: **keine.**

>> An average person, a tramp and a show-off are comparing what they own.

> Der Normalbürger: Ich habe ein Haus.
> Der Penner: Ich habe kein Haus.
> Der Angeber: Ich habe sechs Häuser.

Write out what they would say with regard to:

1 das Hemd
2 das Auto
3 das Radio
4 das Motorrad
5 die Flasche Wein
6 das Wörterbuch
7 die Jacke

3.2 Possessives

meine Freundin	unsere Sachen
unser Flaschenöffner	eure Sachen

○ The German possessives are:

mein	*my*
dein	*your (familiar sing.)*
sein	*his*
ihr	*her; their*
Ihr	*your (formal; sing. and pl.)*
unser	*our*
euer	*your (familiar pl.)*

○ All these are like **ein** in that they have no ending in masculine and neuter singular. (The **-er** in **unser** and **euer** is not an ending, it is part of the word itself!). For the feminine and plural, they add an **-e**.

mein Vater	*my father*
meine Mutter	*my mother*
unser Flaschenöffner	*our bottle-opener*
unsere Sachen	*our things*

○ Note that the difference between **sein** and **ihr** depends as in English on the owner, not on the thing owned. But the ending will depend on the item owned, i.e.

sein Vater	*his father*
ihr Vater	*her father*
seine Mutter	*his mother*
ihre Mutter	*her mother*

》 Rewrite the following phrases putting into German the words in italics:

1 Das ist (*my*) Freund.
2 Hier ist (*your, familiar sing*) Flaschenöffner.
3 Kommen (*your, familiar plural*) Vorfahren aus Deutschland?
4 Ist das (*her*) Zelt?
5 Wo sind (*our*) Sachen?
6 Wie ist (*your, formal*) Name?
7 Kennst du schon (*my*) Freundin?
8 Hans stellt Elfriede vor; sie ist (*his*) Schwägerin.
9 Hans and Peter kommen. Ich höre schon (*their*) Auto.

Meine sechs Motorräder

3.3 Determiners in the accusative

> Hast du unseren Flaschenöffner gesehen?
> es gibt einen Sachsen

- First, remind yourself of the main uses of the accusative (section 1.6).

- So far, we have met the definite and indefinite article, the words **dieser**, **jeder** etc. and the possessives. A useful single term to describe all these is ***determiners***. This refers to the fact that they determine which person or thing you are talking about.

- In German, determiners have an accusative form only in the masculine singular. Feminines, neuters and plurals do not change in the accusative.

The accusative forms of the most common determiners are:

Nominative	Accusative	Nominative	Accusative
der	**den**	**mein**	**meinen**
dieser	**diesen**	**dein**	**deinen**
jeder	**jeden**	**sein**	**seinen**
ein	**einen**	**ihr**	**ihren**
kein	**keinen**	**Ihr**	**Ihren**
		unser	**unseren**
		euer	**euren**

- For English-speaking learners of German, the main problem with the accusative is in identifying whether a particular noun is the object of the verb or not. With pronouns, this problem does not arise, since English also has accusative pronouns (*me, him,* etc.) But English does not have a separate accusative form for determiners.

The object of the verb is the person or thing directly affected by the action, and if this is a masculine singular noun, German will use an accusative determiner. In the question:

Have you seen our bottle-opener?

the subject is *you* and the object is *bottle-opener*. So in German:

Hast du unseren Flaschenöffner gesehen?

41

But if the question had been:

Where is our bottle-opener?

then *bottle-opener* is the subject, so no accusative is required:

Wo ist unser Flaschenöffner?

A helpful rule of thumb is that no accusatives are required after the verbs **sein** (*to be*), **(er)scheinen** (*to appear*), **bleiben** (*to remain*) or after **werden** when used on its own to mean *to become*:

Er ist mein Bruder. *He is my brother.*
Er bleibt mein Freund. *He is still my friend.*

A» In the following sentences, some of the nouns are masculine, some are feminine and some are neuter. Decide which is which, and then add the appropriate ending (if any!) to the determiner.

1 Sie suchen ein___ Zeltplatz.
2 Wo hat er sein___ Auto geparkt?
3 Hast du mein___ Bluse gesehen?
4 Hast du unser___ Flaschenöffner gesehen?
5 Wir müssen unser___ Abendessen vorbereiten.
6 Unsere Zeltnachbarn suchen ihr___ Autopapiere.
7 Kennst du mein___ Freund Hans?

B» Now decide which of the following masculines is an object and which is not. Then complete the determiner as before.

1 D___ Student schreibt d___ Brief.
2 Wo ist d___ Brief?
3 D___ Student ist d___ Bruder von Carla.
4 D___ Student ist ein___ Freund von mir.
5 In Alzey hat Susan d___ Wein probiert.
6 Elfriede und Karl trinken ihr___ Wein auch sehr gern.
7 Das Weingut ist ein___ Familienbetrieb.

C» Complete the second sentence in each pair.

e.g. Das ist der Traktor. Ich fahre den Traktor.

1 Das ist der Wein. Ich trinke _____
2 Das sind die Trauben. Ich schneide _____
3 Das sind die Körbe. Die Männer tragen _____
4 Das ist das Auto. Hans fährt _____
5 Das ist der Flaschenöffner. Die Mädchen suchen _____

3.4 Determiners in the dative

> von seiner Familie   von ihren Familien
> bei deinen Klamotten

○ You have met the main uses of the dative case in section 1.7. The dative forms of the main determiners in German are:

Nominative	Dative Masculine and Neuter	Dative Feminine	Dative Plural
der	**dem**	**der**	**den -n**
dieser	**diesem**	**dieser**	**diesen -n**
jeder	**jedem**	**jeder**	**-**
ein	**einem**	**einer**	**-**
kein	**keinem**	**keiner**	**keinen -n**
mein	**meinem**	**meiner**	**meinen -n**
dein	**deinem**	**deiner**	**deinen -n**
sein	**seinem**	**seiner**	**seinen -n**
ihr	**ihrem**	**ihrer**	**ihren -n**
Ihr	**Ihrem**	**Ihrer**	**Ihren -n**
unser	**unserem**	**unserer**	**unseren -n**
euer	**eurem**	**eurer**	**euren -n**

○ The additional **-n** in the plural is added to the noun itself provided that this does not already end in an **-n** or in an **-s** (which would make an additional **-n** very hard to pronounce).

Nominative singular	**der Freund**
Dative singular	**dem Freund**
Nominative plural	**die Freunde**
Dative plural	**den Freunden**

But **die Lampen,** for example, already has an **-n**, so no more can be added, and the dative plural of **das Auto** is **den Autos.**

○ In some set phrases and in German written some time ago, you will find an **-e** added to the dative singular of nouns, e.g.

    zu Hause   *at home*

A》 In the following statements about our story so far, substitute the appropriate dative determiner for the English word in italics.

1 Susan wohnt bei (*her*) Freundin in Deutschland.
2 Alle helfen bei (*the*) Weinlese.
3 Elfriede zahlt (*the*) Helfern einen guten Lohn.
4 Die Weinkönigin empfiehlt (*her*) Gästen den Alzeyer Wein.
5 Rüdiger erzählt von (*his*) Familie.
6 Carla zeigt (*her*) Freundin, wo der Flaschenöffner ist.
7 Die Mädchen bieten (*their*) Gästen ein schönes Abendessen an.

B》 In the following, substitute the words in brackets with a plural.

e.g. Carla zeigt (ihrem Gast) den Zeltplatz.
Carla zeigt ihren Gästen den Zeltplatz.

1 Elfriede bäckt (dem Arbeiter) Kuchen für den Nachmittag.
2 Karl dankt (dem Helfer).
3 Rüdiger erklärt (dem Nachbarn) seine Familiengeschichte.
4 Der Flaschenöffner gehört (dem Mädchen).
5 Susan schickt (ihre Freundin eine Ansichtskarte) von Alzey.
6 Der Pole and die Ungarin helfen (dem Winzer) bei der Weinlese.

Die Weinkönigin empfiehlt den Alzeyer Wein

3.5. Determiners in the genitive

> ich wusste den Namen seiner Firma
> eine Branche meiner Familie

○ In English, we can say *the girl's friends* or *the friends of the girl*. Spoken German tends to express possession by using **von** and the dative; but written German usually uses the *genitive*.

Ich wusste den Namen seiner Firma.
I knew the name of his firm.

der Vater meines Freundes
the father of my friend; my friend's father

○ There are also a few prepositions which are followed by the genitive. The most important are:

statt *instead of*   **während** *during*
trotz *in spite of*   **wegen** *because of*

○ The forms of the genitive are:

Nominative	Genitive Masculine and Neuter	Genitive Feminine and Plural
der	**des** -(e)s	**der**
dieser	**dieses** -(e)s	**dieser**
jeder	**jedes** -(e)s	**jeder** (no plural)
ein	**eines** -(e)s	**einer** (no plural)
kein	**keines** -(e)s	**keiner**
mein	**meines** -(e)s	**meiner**
dein	**deines** -(e)s	**deiner**
sein	**seines** -(e)s	**seiner**
ihr	**ihres** -(e)s	**ihrer**
Ihr	**Ihres** -(e)s	**Ihrer**
unser	**unseres** -(e)s	**unserer**
euer	**eures** -(e)s	**eurer**

○ In the masculine and neuter, the noun itself adds an **-s** or **-es** depending on which is easier to pronounce. Dictionaries show this genitive ending before the plural ending, but the general rules on the following page apply:

45

Nouns of more than one syllable or ending in a vowel add **-s**:

des Lehrers   **des Autos**

Nouns ending in **-s**, **-ß**, **-ss**, **-sch** or **-z** add **-es**:

des Hauses   **des Tisches**

Other nouns of only one syllable add **-es** in formal written German but frequently only **-s** in speech and informal writing:

des Buches or **des Buchs**
des Tages or **des Tags**

>> Write out the following examples giving the correct genitive form of the words in brackets:

1   Die Qualität _____ ist dieses Jahr sehr gut. (*der Wein*)
2   Die Nachbarn _____ helfen bei der Weinlese. (*die Familie*)
3   Das Haus _____ ist sehr groß. (*meine Eltern*)
4   Die Freundin _____ ist älter als ich. (*mein Bruder*)
5   Die Geschichte _____ ist sehr interessant. (*deine Vorfahren*)
6   Ich habe den Namen _____ vergessen. (*diese Stadt*)
7   Während _____ haben Karl und Elfriede viel Arbeit. (*der Sommer*)

3.6 Weak nouns

ich wusste den Namen   es gibt einen Sachsen

○   About 10% of masculine nouns in German have an **-(e)n** ending in the plural and in the accusative, dative and genitive singular. These are called weak nouns.

e.g.   Nom   **der Student**
       Acc   **den Studenten**
       Dat   **dem Studenten**
       Gen   **des Studenten**
       Plural   **die Studenten**

○ The most important nouns in this group are:

Nouns ending in **-e**, including several which denote nationality or regional origin, e.g. **der Franzose, der Sachse** and **der Kunde** *customer*.

Imported nouns especially those ending in **-and**, **-ant**, **-ent**, **-ist**, **-krat**, **-nom**, e.g. **der Komponist, der Demokrat**.

A smaller number of nouns of German origin not ending in **-e**. Among the most common are:

der Bayer *Bavarian*	**der Held** *hero*
der Graf *count*	**der Nachbar** *neighbour*

○ There are a few irregular variations worth learning:

der Herr has an **-n** ending in the singular, but **-en** in the plural
der Name has the usual endings but a genitive **des Namens**;
der Buchstabe *letter* and **der Glaube** *faith* behave in the same way.

A⟩⟩ In the following, supply the correct form for the words in brackets:

1   Elfriede hat viele (*Kunde*).
2   Der (*Kunde*) ist für sie sehr wichtig.
3   Sie schreibt (*der Kunde*) einen Brief.
4   Kennen Sie (*der Student*) aus Polen?
5   Kennen Sie (*der Name/dieser Herr*)?
6   Ist das das Zelt (*der Sachse*)?

B⟩⟩ To revise many of the main points in this Unit, complete the following summary by translating the words in italics:

Karl und Elfriede haben (*a vineyard*) in Alzey. Karl erzählt Susan von (*his work*) und sie probieren (*the wine*). Karl und Elfriede arbeiten zusammen mit der Winzergenossenschaft und sie verkaufen (*their wines*) in alle Welt. Das Weingut ist (*a family firm*) und alle (*members of the family*) helfen bei (*the wine harvest*). Susan und Carla finden (*a campsite*) in der Nähe von Alzey und sprechen mit (*a neighbour*). Carla kann (*the bottle-opener*) nicht finden, er liegt bei (*her*) Klamotten!

Summary: the case endings

	Masculine	Neuter	Feminine	Plural
Nominative	der	das	die	die
	dieser	dieses	diese	diese
	ein	ein	eine	-
	kein	kein	keine	keine
	mein	mein	meine	meine
	Ihr	Ihr	Ihre	Ihre
	unser	unser	unsere	unsere
Accusative	den	as above	as above	as above
	diesen			
	einen			
	keinen			
	meinen			
	Ihren			
	unseren			
Dative	dem	dem	der	den -n
	diesem	diesem	dieser	diesen -n
	einem	einem	einer	-
	keinem	keinem	keiner	keinen -n
	meinem	meinem	meiner	meinen -n
	Ihrem	Ihrem	Ihrer	Ihren -n
	unserem	unserem	unserer	unseren -n
Genitive	des -s	des -s	der	der
	dieses -s	dieses -s	dieser	dieser
	eines -s	eines -s	einer	-
	keines -s	keines -s	keiner	keiner
	meines -s	meines -s	meiner	meiner
	Ihres -s	Ihres -s	Ihrer	Ihrer
	unseres -s	unseres -s	unserer	unserer

The uses of the cases

Nominative

- For the subject of the sentence, i.e. the person doing the action
- After verbs *to be, to seem, to appear* etc.
- After **so ... wie** (*as ... as*) and **als** (*than*)

Accusative

- For the object of the sentence, the person or thing affected by the action of the verb
- After prepositions **durch, für, gegen, ohne** and **um**
- After prepositions of motion (see section 5.4)

Dative

- For the indirect object of the verb, the person (or sometimes the thing) advantaged by the action; especially after verbs like **geben, erzählen, danken, zeigen**
- After prepositions **aus, bei, mit, nach, seit, von, zu**
- After prepositions of location (see section 5.4)

Genitive

- For the owner of something
- After prepositions **statt, trotz, während, wegen**

4 Saying how many and when

Omas achtzigster Geburtstag

Der Geburtstag

Hans, Carla und Susan sind zur Geburtstagsfeier der Großmutter eingeladen. Geburtstag ist in Deutschland ein wichtiger Tag, besonders wenn es ein „Nuller" ist. In Alzey feiert die Oma ihren **achtzigsten** Geburtstag   4.2

Hans   Fahrt ihr mit zum Geburtstag meiner Oma nach Alzey? Sie wird **am 28. September achtzig**. Da gibt   4.5 / 4.1
es viele Kuchen und viel Betrieb. Eingeladen haben wir niemanden, aber es werden so **sechzig** bis   4.1
siebzig Leute kommen. Ich schätze, über **50 Prozent**   4.1 / 4.3
sprechen Dialekt! Da muss Susan sich anstrengen!

Carla   Sollen wir mit dem Zug fahren? Das geht sehr
schnell und dauert nur **anderthalb** Stunden. Mit   4.3
dem Zug **um 12 Uhr** kommen wir zeitig an.   4.4

Susan	**Punkt 12 Uhr** geht ein Zug?	4.4
Carla	Nein, der geht um **Viertel nach zwölf**, genauer gesagt um 12.17 Uhr.	4.4
Hans	Was kostet das? Für drei wird das doch viel teurer als mit dem Auto, oder?	
Carla	Mit unseren BahnCards können wir ganz preiswert fahren.	
Hans	Aber ich brauche nur **20 Liter Benzin**, das kostet höchstens **ein Drittel**. Und dann können wir am Samstag nach Bad Dürkheim fahren und auf den Wurstmarkt gehen. Den Wurstmarkt feiert man **jedes Jahr um den ersten Oktober**. Er dauert eine ganze Woche. Man kann sogar in einem riesigen Weinfass Wein trinken.	4.6 4.3 4.7 / 4.5
Susan	Also fahren wir mit dem Auto. Wie viele Kilometer sind es?	
Carla	Ungefähr **hundertvierzig Kilometer**. Wann sollen wir da sein? Fahren wir **gegen ein Uhr** hier in Frankfurt ab?	4.1 4.4
Hans	In Ordnung. Ich komme um **zirka ein Uhr** und dann fahren wir sofort los. Wir kommen dann etwa um **halb drei** an.	4.7 4.4
Carla	Was nehmen wir als Geschenk mit?	
Hans	Es braucht nicht allzu viel zu kosten. Oma legt nicht viel Wert auf Geschenke. Ich habe ihr einen Schal gekauft. Wie wäre es mit **ein paar Blumen** oder **einer Schachtel Pralinen**?	4.7 4.6

4.1 Cardinal numbers

sechzig   siebzig
achtzig   hundertvierzig Kilometer

○ We use the term **cardinal numbers** to indicate simple numbers like *three, twenty-five, one hundred and thirty* etc., and **ordinal numbers** to indicate the descriptions *third, twenty-fifth, one hundred and thirtieth,* etc.

In German the cardinal numbers are:

1	eins	11	elf
2	zwei	12	zwölf
3	drei	13	dreizehn
4	vier	14	vierzehn
5	fünf	15	fünfzehn
6	sechs	16	sechzehn
7	sieben	17	siebzehn
8	acht	18	achtzehn
9	neun	19	neunzehn
10	zehn		

Note that the **s** is dropped in **sechzehn** and the **en** in **siebzehn!**

○ The tens are:

20	zwanzig	60	sechzig
30	dreißig	70	siebzig
40	vierzig	80	achtzig
50	fünfzig	90	neunzig

Note that the **s** is again dropped in **sechzig** and the **en** in **siebzig,** and that **dreißig** is the only one not written with a **z**.

○ Numbers after 20 are formed with **-und-**

21	einundzwanzig
24	vierundzwanzig

○ Numbers over 100 are almost always written in figures, but sometimes have to be spoken out loud. On the rare occasions when they are written out, all numbers below a million are written as a single word.

100	**(ein)hundert**
101	**hundert(und)eins**
130	**hundertdreißig**
734	**siebenhundertvierunddreißig**
6 539	**sechstausendfünfhundertneununddreißig**
506 834	**fünfhundertundsechstausendachthundert-** **vierunddreißig**

Note that there is no comma between the thousands and the hundreds, merely a short space.

If numbers over a million are are ever written out in full, the words are separated:

3 400 000 **drei Millionen vierhunderttausend**

○ Years are written in numerals without the 'thousands' space. Dates from the eleventh and twenty-first centuries are spoken with thousands:

1066	**tausendsechsundsechzig**
2004	**zweitausendvier**

Dates from all other centuries are spoken with hundreds:

1978 **neunzehnhundertachtundsiebzig.**

Note that you can either say just the year or preface it with **im Jahre**. You cannot simply use **in** as you would in English. So *in 1872* is either **im Jahre 1872** or simply **1872.**

Columbus hat 1492 Amerika entdeckt.
Columbus discovered America in 1492.

○ Distances are written out and spoken as follows:

37 m	**siebenunddreißig Meter**
140 km	**hundertvierzig Kilometer**

○ Other points worth noting about numbers are:

The form **zwo** rather than **zwei** is commonly used on the telephone (to avoid confusion of zwei and drei) and increasingly in everyday speech for emphasis.

Eine Milliarde (1 000 000 000) is a thousand million and is very commonly used.

The indefinite large number, equivalent to English *umpteen* is **zig**.

Wir kennen uns schon zig Jahre
We've known each other for umpteen years.

○ In handwriting the numeral 7 is always crossed with a stroke to distinguish it from the figure 1.

A⟩⟩ Here are some facts about the family in Alzey and a question. Read them out loud, then answer the question in German.

Elfriede wird dieses Jahr 51 Jahre alt. Die Großmutter wird 80. Hans ist fast 30.

Wie viel älter ist die Großmutter als Hans und Elfriede?

B⟩⟩ The following are short descriptions of geographical facts and the history of the potato and the banana. Again, read them out loud, then write out in full the numbers and years.

1   Mount Everest ist mit 8 848 m der höchste Berg der Welt. Die Zugspitze ist mit 2 963 m der höchste Berg Deutschlands. Die Wolga ist mit 3 700 km der längste Fluss Europas.

2   Sir Francis Drake hat im Jahre 1586 den Genuss der Kartoffel in Europa verbreitet. Es dauerte aber noch über 200 Jahre, bis Friedrich der Große die Kartoffel auch in Deutschland einführte.

3   1892 wurde die Banane von Richard Lehman per Schiff zum ersten Mal nach Deutschland gebracht. Fast 100 Jahre später wurde die Banane fast zur Symbolfrucht der deutschen Einheit, denn 44 Jahre lang (von 1945 bis 1989) gab es in der DDR nur sehr selten Bananen. Ein Jahr nach der Vereinigung, also 1991, lag der Pro-Kopf-Verbrauch im Osten mit 25 Kilo weit über dem im Westen. Die „Wessis" aßen in diesem Jahr 14 kg pro Kopf.

4.2 Ordinal numbers

> Sie feiert ihren achtzigsten Geburtstag.

○ The ordinal numbers *first* to *nineteenth* are formed with the ending **-te**. In numerals, this is expressed with a full stop.

1.	der erste	11.	der elfte
2.	der zweite	12.	der zwölfte
3.	der dritte	13.	der dreizehnte
4.	der vierte	14.	der vierzehnte
5.	der fünfte	15.	der fünfzehnte
6.	der sechste	16.	der sechzehnte
7.	der siebte	17.	der siebzehnte
8.	der achte	18.	der achtzehnte
9.	der neunte	19.	der neunzehnte
10.	der zehnte		

The only irregular forms here are **der erste**, **der dritte** and **der siebte**.

○ From *twentieth* onwards, the ending **-ste** is added. There are no exceptions:

80. **der achtzigste**
352. **der dreihundertzweiundfünfzigste**

○ The article will, of course, vary according to gender:

der achtzigste Geburtstag
die zweite Reise
das vierte Kind

The ending on the ordinal will depend on case; in the nominative it is usually **-e**, in the accusative (masculine only), dative and genitive it is **-en:**

Der erste Zug ist schon abgefahren.
Er nimmt den zweiten Zug.

Only if there is no ending on the determiner (i.e. after **ein, mein, sein, ihr** etc. — see sections 3.1 and 3.2) will the ending on the ordinal be **-er** for masculines and **-es** for neuters.

> **mein zwanzigster Geburtstag**
> **ihr viertes Kind**

>> In the following examples, substitute the correct German for the English ordinal given in italics:

1 Der (*first*) Mann auf dem Mond war Neil Armstrong.
2 König Ludwig (*the Second*) hat viele Schlösser in Deutschland gebaut.
3 Der FC Bayern München wurde 1999 zum (*fifteenth*) Mal deutscher Meister.
4 Mit dem Jahr 2000 begann das (*twenty-first*) Jahrhundert.
5 1988 wurde der Nobelpreis für Chemie zum (*twenty-third*) Mal an deutsche Chemiker verliehen.

4.3 Fractions

ein Drittel	anderthalb	50 Prozent

○ With the exception of **die Hälfte** (*half*), all the fractions in German are neuter nouns adding **-l** to the ordinal numbers:

> **der dritte ... (Mann)**   *the third ... (man)*
> **ein Drittel**   *one third*
> **ein Viertel**   *a quarter*
> **ein Zwanzigstel**   *a twentieth*

○ German decimal fractions are written with a comma rather than a point, so the spoken form is ... **Komma** ...:

> **5,7**   **fünf Komma sieben**
> *5.7*   *five point seven*

The word for *percent is* **Prozent:**

> **70%   siebzig Prozent**
> **38,4%   achtunddreißig Komma vier Prozent**

○   Note the following expressions with fractions:

> **anderthalb**   *one and a half*
> **dreieinhalb**   *three and a half*

A》 You should not need much mathematics to complete the following, but you will need to show you understand how fractions are expressed in German!

1   Elfriede hat für die Geburtstagsfeier eine Sahnetorte gebacken. Sie teilt sie in zwölf Stücke; jedes Stück ist also ein _____ von der Torte.

2   Sie hat auch eine Schwarzwälder Kirschtorte gebacken. Die ist größer, also kann man sie in zwanzig Teile schneiden. Jedes Stück ist diesmal ein _____.

3   100g Quark hat 15g Fettgehalt. Die Magerstufe hat nur 7g Fettgehalt pro 100g, also hat sie nur die _____ Fettgehalt.

4   Oma hat fünfzehn Urenkel und hat ihnen zu Weihnachten Geld geschenkt. Jeder hat den gleichen Anteil bekommen, also ein

_____.

B》 The following table shows the percentage of foreigners living in German cities at the turn of the millennium. Read the list out loud, then write out the percentages in full.

e.g.   München 20,1
        In München wohnen zwanzig Komma eins Prozent Ausländer.

1   Frankfurt   28,5
2   Ludwigshafen   19,9
3   Düsseldorf   16,3
4   Münster   8,1

Now express the same figures as approximate fractions.

e.g. In München sind es ungefähr ein Fünftel, etc.

Use your pocket calculator if you have to!

4.4 Times

um zwölf Uhr	halb drei	12.17 Uhr
gegen ein Uhr	Punkt 12 Uhr	Viertel nach zwölf

○ The 24-hour clock is used in official, written and increasingly in spoken German. Times are written out followed by the word **Uhr**, but spoken with the word **Uhr** between the hours and the minutes. e.g **5.27 Uhr** spoken as **fünf Uhr siebenundzwanzig**.

○ The 12-hour clock is still used extensively in conversational German. The five-minute points are:

3.00	**drei Uhr**
3.05	**fünf nach drei**
3.10	**zehn nach drei**
3.15	**Viertel nach drei**
3.20	**zwanzig nach drei**
3.25	**fünf vor halb vier**
3.30	**halb vier**
3.35	**fünf nach halb vier**
3.40	**zwanzig vor vier**
3.45	**Viertel vor vier**
3.50	**zehn vor vier**
3.55	**fünf vor vier**

Points worth noting in the above are:

From as early as 25 past the hour, attention focuses on the coming hour, not the one just past.

Especially in Southern Germany, you may also encounter:

> **viertel vier** rather than **Viertel nach drei,** and
> **drei viertel vier** rather than **Viertel vor vier.**

(Note that **Viertel**, being a noun, is normally written with a capital V, but not in these last two examples which — since the recent spelling reforms — are exceptions.)

Individual minutes are spoken with the insertion of the word **Minuten,** much as in English:

3.07	**sieben Minuten nach drei**
3.53	**sieben Minuten vor vier**

○ The German equivalents of the most common English words used in time phrases are:-

at	**um**
around	**gegen**
from ... to	**von ... bis**
exactly	**Punkt**

The parts of the day are:

morgens/vormittags
mittags
(around mid-day; also used in the afternoon)
nachmittags
abends
nachts

Noon is **zwölf Uhr mittags**
Midnight is **Mitternacht** or **null Uhr** or **zwölf Uhr nachts**

>> Read aloud and write out the following times, giving as many alternatives as you can for each (use both the 12-hour and the 24-hour clock),

e.g. 13.45 Uhr: dreizehn Uhr fünfundvierzig, Viertel vor zwei (nachmittags), drei viertel zwei (nachmittags)

1 9.10 Uhr	**4** 11.15 Uhr	**7** 12.25 Uhr	**10** 12.30 Uhr
2 14.35 Uhr	**5** 15.40 Uhr	**8** 17.45 Uhr	**11** 19.55 Uhr
3 20.57 Uhr	**6** 00.03 Uhr	**9** 12.17 Uhr	**12** 17.38 Uhr

Zwölf Uhr mittags

4.5 Dates

am achtundzwanzigsten September
um den ersten Oktober

○ The days and months in German are:

Days	Months
Montag	**Januar**
Dienstag	**Februar**
Mittwoch	**März**
Donnerstag	**April**
Freitag	**Mai**
Samstag OR	**Juni**
Sonnabend	**Juli**
Sonntag	**August**
	September
	Oktober
	November
	Dezember

Sonnabend is used mainly in northern Germany, but both names for Saturday are widespread throughout the country and virtually interchangeable.

First used on the telephone to avoid possible confusion between **Juni** and **Juli,** the alternatives **Juno** and **Julei** are increasingly being used in spoken German.

○ For the date in the month, the ordinal number **(der erste, der zweite)** is used as in English:

> **der erste November**
> **der vierundzwanzigste Oktober**

(Always masculine, because **der Tag** is masculine and **der erste** is short for **der erste Tag.)**

In writing this is expressed either as:

der 1. November   OR   **1.11.**
der 24. Oktober   OR   **24.10.**

In letter-writing, it is usual to put the date in the accusative at the top right, often with the place of writing, e.g:

Hamburg, den 23. September 2001

○ On the other hand, most prepositions used in connection with time require the dative:

on the	**an dem**, shortened to **am**
since the	**seit dem**
from the ... to the	**von dem ... bis zu dem**
	shortened to **vom ... bis zum**

The dative -**n** on the ordinal itself (see section 4.2) is only evident when the date is spoken or written out in full:

am 21. Dezember
spoken **am einundzwanzigsten Dezember**
on the 21st December

seit dem 19. März
spoken **seit dem neunzehnten März**
since the 19th March

vom 13. bis zum 17. Juni
spoken **vom dreizehnten bis zum siebzehnten Juni**
from the 13th to the 17th June

A>> The following is a description of the main festivals of the year in Germany. Write out in full all the dates (and the time) mentioned.

Am 1.1. (**1**) ist Neujahr, am 6.1. (**2**) der Dreikönigstag. Die Faschingszeit beginnt am 11.11. (**3**) um 11.11 Uhr (**4**) und endet am Tag vor Aschermittwoch. Ostern ist ein bewegliches Fest zwischen dem 22.3. (**5**) und dem 25.4. (**6**). Pfingsten ist am siebten Sonntag nach Ostern. Zwischendurch feiert man aber den 1.5. (**7**) als Tag der Arbeit. Früher feierte man den 17. 6. (**8**) in Erinnerung an den Aufstand in Ostdeutschland 1953 (**9**), aber heutzutage feiert man den 3.10. (**10**) als Tag der Deutschen Einheit. Protestanten feiern am 31.10. (**11**) das Reformationsfest, Katholiken am 1.11. (**12**) Allerheiligen und am 2.11. (**13**) Allerseelen. Am 6.12. (**14**) ist Nikolaustag, am 24.12. (**15**) Heiligabend. Der 25.12. (**16**) und der 26.12. (**17**) sind die Weihnachtsfeiertage. Silvester, am 31.12. (**18**), ist der letzte Tag im Jahr.

B>> The dramatic events of 1989 moved very fast; it seems incredible that so much could happen in such a short space of time. In the following summary, translate into German the English dates given in italics.

On 2nd May (**1**) begann Ungarn mit dem Abbau der Grenze zu Österreich. *On 24th August* (**2**) verließen 108 Deutsche aus der DDR die Budapester Botschaft der Bundesrepublik mit Papieren des Internationalen Roten Kreuzes. Ungarn öffnete *on 11th September* (**3**) für DDR-Bürger die Grenze nach Österreich. In Leipzig demonstrierten *on 2nd October* (**4**) 20 000 Menschen für Reformen in der DDR. *The 7th October* (**5**) war der Jahrestag der DDR, und es fand eine große Militärparade statt. Der Staatsratsvorsitzende Erich Honecker trat *on 18th October* (**6**) zurück; sein Nachfolger war Egon Krenz. Die größte Demonstration in Ostberlin fand *on 4th November* (**7**) mit mindestens 500 000 Teilnehmern statt. Die Regierung trat *on 7th November* (**8**) zurück und zwei Tage später, *on 9th November* (**9**), wurden die Berliner Mauer und die Grenze zu Westdeutschland geöffnet.

4.6 Expressions of quantity

eine Schachtel Pralinen   20 Liter Benzin

○ The important point to note with regard to expressions of quantity
is that there is no equivalent in German to the English *of.*

> *20 litres of petrol is* simply **20 Liter Benzin**
> and *a box of chocolates* is **eine Schachtel Pralinen.**

Weights and liquids are measured in metric quantities; a simple rule
of thumb is that a pint is just over half a **Liter** and there are
approximately two pounds to a **Kilo;** in fact spoken German often
uses **das Pfund** meaning half a Kilo.

A⟩⟩ Susan is so impressed with Elfriede's Sachertorte (an Austrian
cake now very popular in Gemany) that she asks her for the
recipe. Here is Susan's note of the ingredients. Can you read it
out loud?

> Zutaten:
> 150 g Schokolade
> 150 g Butter
> 150 g Zucker
> 1 gestrichener Teelöffel Backpulver
> 6 Eier
> 30 g Puderzucker
> 150 g Mehl
> Aprikosenkuvertüre

B⟩⟩ Translate the following expressions into German:

1   10 apples
2   1 jar (glass) of jam
3   1 box of chocolates
4   2 lb coffee
5   1 bottle of wine

4.7 Other expressions of time and number

jedes Jahr   ein paar Blumen

O   The following expressions of time and number are worth learning:

heute früh / heute Morgen	*this morning*
heute Nachmittag	*this afternoon*
morgen	*tomorrow*
morgen früh	*tomorrow morning*
übermorgen	*the day after tomorrow*
gestern	*yesterday*
gestern Abend	*yesterday evening (last night)*
vorgestern	*the day before yesterday*
täglich	*daily*
Tag für Tag	*day in, day out*
jeden Tag	*every day*
jedes Jahr	*every year*
einmal	*once*
zweimal	*twice*
jedes Mal	*every time*
manchmal	*sometimes*
zigmal / x-mal	*countless times*
diesmal	*this time*
zum ersten Mal	*for the first time*
zum zweiten Mal	*for the second time*
vorläufig	*for the time being*
rechtzeitig	*on time, in good time*
in diesem Moment	*just at that moment*
zur Zeit	*just now, for the time being*
ungefähr / zirka	*about*
knapp	*just on*
zweierlei	*two kinds of*
ein paar	*a few*
ein Paar	*a pair, a couple*

○ The word **seit** is used to express how long something has been going on. The verb is in the present tense if what you are describing is still going on, and in the simple past (see section 7.6) if you are talking only about the past.

e.g. **Ich wohne seit zwanzig Jahren in London.**
I have been living in London for twenty years.

A⟩⟩ Use 'seit' to relate the following sentences to the present time:

e.g. Heute vor 30 Jahren haben wir geheiratet.
Wir sind seit 30 Jahren verheiratet.

1   Susan ist vor einer Woche in Frankfurt angekommen.
2   Die Familie hat diesen Weinberg vor drei Generationen übernommen.
3   Vor fünf Jahren habe ich bei Siemens begonnen.
4   Die Großmutter wurde vor 80 Jahren in Alzey geboren.
5   Ich habe vor fünf Jahren aufgehört, Kaffee zu trinken.

B⟩⟩ The following is an account of a worker with a problem. Write it out in full, translating into German the English phrases in italics.

(**1** *Day in, day out*) stehe ich um sieben Uhr auf. (**2** *Every day*) fahre ich mit dem Auto zur Arbeit. (**3** *This morning*) ist es anders. (**4** *Last night*) habe ich nämlich gefeiert and ich kann (**5** *this morning*) nicht aufstehen. (**6** *This time*) muß ich aber bei der Firma anrufen. (**7** *Just at this moment*) läutet das Telefon. Es ist mein Chef. „(**8** *For the third time*) sind Sie nicht (**9** *on time*) zur Arbeit gekommen. (**10** *Just now*) haben wir so viel Arbeit. Sie müssen sofort kommen." Immer, wenn ich schwänzen will, merkt es der Chef!

5 Saying where things are

Die Studentenbude

Roswitha, die Tochter von Karl und Elfriede, studiert in
Frankfurt. Sie hat ein Zimmer bei Frau Siebert in Bornheim.
Auf der Geburtstagsfeier erzählt sie Susan **von ihrem**
Zimmer.

5.1 / 5.9

Susan	Was für ein Zimmer hast du in Frankfurt?
Roswitha	Das Zimmer ist nicht sehr groß. Mein Schreibtisch steht **vor dem Fenster. Auf dem Schreibtisch** ist mein Computer

5.4

Susan	Du hast einen Computer?
Roswitha	Natürlich, den muss man haben. Ich schreibe alle Seminararbeiten auf dem Computer. Das ist viel leichter, man kann dann seine Fehler verbessern.
Susan	Hast du auch einen Drucker?
Roswitha	Selbstverständlich. Der Drucker steht **unter dem Tisch** and gleich **daneben** ist der Papierkorb, in den ich meinen Abfall werfen kann.

5.4
5.8

Susan	**Wo stellst du denn deinen Computer hin**, wenn du **mit der Arbeit** fertig bist?

5.7
5.3

Roswitha	Ich habe einen Laptop und **nach der Arbeit** stelle ich ihn **auf das Regal** neben dem Tisch. Über diesem Regal hängt ein Poster.

5.3
5.4

Susan	**In meinem Zimmer** nimmt das Bett den meisten Platz ein.

5.4

Roswitha	Bei mir auch. Mein Bett steht links. **Darunter** ist mein Koffer. **Neben dem Bett** ist ein Schränkchen. **Darauf** stehen mein Wecker und der CD-Spieler. Meine Kleider hänge ich **in den Kleiderschrank** neben dem Bett.

5.8
5.4
5.8
5.4

Susan	Ist dein Zimmer weit **von der Universität**?	5.3
Roswitha	Ich kann in zwanzig Minuten **hinfahren**. Zuerst	5.7
	gehe ich **durch den Grünburgpark zur Haltestelle**.	5.2 / 5.6
	Dann fahre ich **mit der U-Bahn** und steige an der	5.1
	Hauptwache um. Noch einmal fünf Minuten	
	die Straße entlang und **schon bin ich da**.	5.4 / 5.7
Susan	Fährst du oft **nach Hause**?	5.1
Roswitha	**Während der Semesterferien** bin ich meist **zu**	5.5 / 5.1
	Hause. Aber **während des Semesters** ist das ein	5.5
	ewiges Hin- und Herfahren. **Mal bin ich hier**, **mal**	5.7
	bin ich dort und was ich suche, ist **immer nicht da**.	5.7
	Das ist dann woanders.	
Susan	Das sagt mein Bruder auch. Er studiert **im**	5.6
	Norden von England. Er möchte auch in	
	Deutschland studieren. Ich glaube, er bekommt	
	das Geld **vom Sokrates-Programm**.	5.6
Roswitha	Ja, es gibt jetzt überall viele Studenten **aus allen**	5.3
	Ländern. Ich glaube, das ist gut. Man lernt andere	
	Leute aus anderen Ländern kennen. Unsere	
	Studenten kommen aus Europa, aus Asien, aus	
	Afrika, einige aus der Schweiz und **aus der Türkei**.	5.3
	Auch aus Südamerika und selbstverständlich	
	auch aus den Vereinigten Staaten.	
Susan	Hast du viele Freunde?	
Roswitha	Wenn man studiert, lernt man immer viele Leute	
	kennen, besonders, wenn man in einem Studenten-	
	wohnheim wohnt. Ich habe Glück, ich wohne	
	privat und ich habe eine sehr nette Nachbarin. Sie	
	ruft mich schon mal **rüber** auf eine Tasse Kaffee.	5.7
Susan	Gut, dass du eine solche Nachbarin hast. **Ohne**	5.2
	Freunde geht's einem schlecht.	

5.1 Flexible meaning of prepositions

> auf der Geburtstagsfeier   mit der U-Bahn
> nach Hause   zu Hause

○ A **preposition** links a noun or pronoun to the rest of the sentence, normally in a phrase which indicates time, place or how an action is done. In English, examples of prepositions are:

> *He got up **at** seven o'clock.*
> *The computer is **on** the table.*
> *Corrections are much easier **with** a computer.*

○ Prepositions are very frequently used words. As a result, a single preposition is often used in several ways, and the way in which this use has evolved in different languages means that there is frequently a mis-match between 'meanings' of prepositions across languages. For example, German **mit** normally corresponds to the English *with*, but for means of transport German uses **mit** where English would normally use *by*.

> Sie fährt **mit** der U-Bahn
> *She goes **by** underground.*

In English you would say:

> ***at** the birthday party*

but in German it is **auf** which normally corresponds to English *on:*

> **auf** der Geburtstagsfeier.

Here are some examples of prepositions in one language with several equivalents in the other:

> German **zu**
>
> **zum** (= zu dem) Rathaus   *to* the Town Hall
> **zu** Weihnachten   *at* Christmas
> **zu** diesem Zweck   *for* this purpose
> **zu** Fuß   *on* foot

English **to**

to the office	**ins** Büro
to the station	**zum** (= zu *dem*) *Bahnhof*
to Germany	**nach** Deutschland
to the Post Office	**auf** die Post
ten to six	zehn **vor** sechs
I'm writing to her.	Ich schreibe **an** sie.

There are also several 'stock phrases' which involve prepositions. Examples in the above dialogue include:

Fährst du oft **nach Hause**?	*Do you often go home?*
Ich bin meist **zu Hause**.	*I am usually at home.*

○ You will probably already know several of the main meanings of German prepositions, even if you have never consciously learnt them. The main point at this stage is to be aware of the problem of multiple meanings, and not to assume that an English preposition will have a single equivalent in German. If in doubt, look it up in a dictionary.

A⟩⟩ In the following examples, decide how you would put the prepositions in italics into English:

1   Das Auto fährt *gegen* die Wand.

2   Ich komme *gegen* sieben Uhr bei euch an.

3   Mein Vater ist sehr *gegen* Rauchen.

4   Wir sitzen *um* den Tisch.

5   Ich komme *um* zwölf Uhr.

6   Wir fahren *nach* Frankfurt.

7   Er kommt erst *nach* sieben Uhr.

8   Wir gehen spät *nach* Hause.

9   Susan kommt *aus* England.

10   Der Stuhl ist *aus* Metall.

11   Ich trinke Bier lieber *aus* dem Glas als *aus* der Flasche.

B》 Choose the appropriate German preposition for each English one in brackets in the following examples:

1 Ich fahre (*to*) Deutschland.
2 Es ist fünf (*to*) sieben.
3 Hans schreibt (*to*) Susan.
4 Susans Vater geht (*to*) sein Büro.
5 Das ist ein Geschenk (*for*) meinen Vater.
6 Er arbeitet (*for*) Ford in Köln.
7 Ich wohne (*for*) zwei Jahren hier.

5.2 Prepositions with accusative

durch den Grünburgpark   ohne Freunde

○ German prepositions determine that the following noun is in a particular case. This may be the accusative, the dative or the genitive. In this section we shall deal first with prepositions which always take the accusative.

○ The six most common of these are:

bis	bis nächsten Freitag	*by/till next Friday*
	bis Hamburg	*as far as Hamburg*
durch	durch den Park	*through the park*
	durch harte Arbeit	*by hard work*
	durch einen Unfall	*due to an accident*
für	für meinen Freund	*for my friend*
	Tag für Tag	*day after day*
gegen	gegen diesen Plan	*against this proposal*
	gegen vier Uhr	*around four o'clock*
	gegen Quittung	*on production of a receipt*
ohne	ohne meinen Mantel	*without my coat*
	ohne Freunde	*without friends*
um	um den Tisch	*round the table*
	um die Ecke	*round the corner*
	um vier Uhr	*at four o'clock*

A» Complete the following account of Roswitha's typical day by replacing the blanks with the appropriate ending:

Jeden Morgen geht Roswitha durch d___ **(1)** Grünburgpark zur U-Bahnhaltestelle. Manchmal kauft sie auf dem Weg belegte Brötchen für sich und für ihr___ **(2)** Freund. Gegen neun Uhr kommt sie in der Universität an. Peter arbeitet nicht weit von der Uni. Oft treffen sie sich gegen zwölf Uhr und essen zusammen zu Mittag. Dienstags und freitags isst sie ohne ihr___ **(3)** Freund. Er hat um dies___ **(4)** Zeit eine Besprechung. Abends gehen sie oft ins Kino, das ist nur um d___ **(5)** Ecke.

B» Below is a list of people for whom Susan wants to buy presents while she is in Germany. Make up a sentence in each case starting with 'Sie braucht ein Geschenk für ...':

1   ihre Mutter
2   ihr Vater
3   ihre Freundin
4   ihr Freund
5   der Onkel in Birmingham
6   die Tante in Manchester

Abends gehen sie oft ins Kino

5.3 Prepositions with dative

| von der Universität | aus allen Ländern | nach der Arbeit |
| aus der Türkei | mit der Arbeit | |

○ The following are common prepositions which always take the dative:

aus	aus dem Fenster	*out of the window*
	aus Hamburg	*from Hamburg*
	aus allen Ländern	*from all countries*
	aus Silber	*(made) of silver*
außer	außer mir	*apart from me*
	außer Atem	*out of breath*
bei	bei Hamburg	*near Hamburg*
	beim (= bei dem)Bäcker	*at the baker's*
	bei ihrer Tante	*at her aunt's*
	bei diesem Gehalt	*for this salary*
	bei einem Glas Wein	*over a glass of wine*
gegenüber	gegenüber dem Rathaus	*opposite the Town Hall*
	dem Rathaus gegenüber	
	(**gegenüber** can precede or follow a noun)	
	mir gegenüber	*opposite me*
	(**gegenüber** always follows a pronoun)	*in relation to me*
mit	mit mir	*with me*
	mit seiner Freundin	*with his girlfriend*
	mit vierzig Jahren	*at the age of forty*
	mit Absicht	*deliberately*
nach	nach Hamburg	*to Hamburg*
	nach meiner Uhr	*by my watch*
	fünf nach zehn	*five past ten*
seit	seit dem Krieg	*since the war*
	seit zehn Jahren	*for ten years*
		(see section 4.7)

von	ein Brief von ihrem Freund	*a letter from her boyfriend*
	zehn Minuten vom	*ten minutes from the*
	(= von dem) Bahnhof	*station*
zu	zum (= zu dem) Bahnhof	*to the station*
	zum Mittagessen	*for lunch*
	10 Briefmarken zu 1 DM	*ten one mark stamps*
	zu Fuß	*on foot*

A⟩⟩ The following is a list of people to whom Susan speaks during her stay in Germany. Write out the full sentence in each case, i.e. 'Susan spricht mit ...'.

1	die Dame	5	der Winzer
2	das Kind	6	seine Frau
3	die Oma	7	der Computerfachmann
4	die Studentin	8	Herr Gruber

Here is a list of things Roswitha tells her about. Start with 'Roswitha erzählt ihr von ... '.

 9 ihr Zimmer
10 das Leben an der Uni
11 die Prüfungen
12 ihr Freund
13 ihre Eltern
14 die Arbeit
15 die Universitätsbibliothek
16 ihr Professor

B⟩⟩ In the following sentences, complete the gaps with the correct dative ending:

1 „Ich komme aus d___ Pfalz", erklärt Roswitha den anderen Studenten.
2 Aus dies___ Buch habe ich die Informationen über das Sokrates-Programm.
3 Von mein___ Eltern bekomme ich ab und zu Taschengeld.
4 „Gehst du zu d___ Vorlesung um acht Uhr?" „Nein, das ist zu früh!".
5 Ich gehe gern mit mein___ Freund abends aus.
6 Von d___ Oma in Alzey bekommt Susan ein schönes Buch.

5.4 Prepositions with accusative or dative

auf das Regal	auf dem Schreibtisch
in den Kleiderschrank	in meinem Zimmer
die Straße entlang	neben dem Bett
unter dem Tisch	vor dem Fenster

○ A number of prepositions can take either the accusative or the dative, depending on the meaning. The most important of these are:

an	**neben**
auf	**über**
entlang	**unter**
hinter	**vor**
in	**zwischen**

The general rule is that where one of these prepositions is used to indicate a direction of movement, it is followed by the accusative. But where it is used to indicate a stationary location, it is followed by the dative.

Some examples:

an
Er geht **an die** Tür.　　　　Er steht **an der** Tür.
He goes to the door.　　　　*He stands at the door.*

auf
Ich stelle ihn **auf das** Regal.　Er steht **auf dem** Regal.
I put it on the shelf.　　　　*It is on the shelf.*

entlang
Roswitha geht **die** Straße　　**Entlang der** Grenze waren
　entlang.　　　　　　　Wachtürme.
Roswitha goes along the street.　*There were watchtowers along*
　　　　　　　　　　　　the border.

(NB **entlang** follows an accusative but precedes a dative.)

hinter
Er geht **hinter die** Kirche.　　**Hinter der** Kirche ist ein
He goes behind the church.　　Friedhof.
　　　　　　　　　　　　Behind the church is a cemetery.

in

Sie hängt die Kleider **in den** Kleiderschrank.
She hangs the clothes in the wardrobe.

Die Kleider hängen **im** Kleiderschrank.
The clothes are hanging in the wardrobe.

neben

Sie stellt das Schränkchen **neben das** Bett.
She puts the cupboard next to the bed.

Neben dem Bett ist das Schränkchen.
The cupboard is next to the bed.

über

Sie hängt den Poster **über das** Regal.
She hangs the poster above the shelf.

Der Poster hängt **über dem** Regal.
The poster is above the shelf.

unter

Sie stellt den Drucker **unter den** Tisch.
She puts the printer under the table.

Der Drucker steht **unter dem** Tisch.
The printer is under the table.

vor

Sie stellt den Schreibtisch **vor das** Fenster.
She puts the table in front of the window.

Der Schreibtisch steht **vor dem** Fenster.
The desk is in front of the window.

zwischen

Sie setzte sich **zwischen meine** Freundin und mich.
She sat down between my girlfriend and me.

Sie saß **zwischen meiner** Freundin und mir.
She was sitting between my girlfriend and me.

○ Note that the accusative is used only if movement in a particular direction is indicated. Thus you can say:

Wir gehen **in die** Stadt.
We go into the town.

(direction indicated)

Wir gehen **in der** Stadt spazieren.
we go for a walk in the town
(no direction indicated)

○ These prepositions are also used in set phrases and expressions which have nothing to do with place. Generally **auf** and **über** take the accusative, the others the dative.

auf diese Weise	*in this way*
auf keinen Fall	*on no account*
ein Buch über die Alpen	*a book about the Alps*
am Sonntag	*on Sunday*
am Ende	*finally*
in der Nacht	*in the night*
im Durchschnitt	*on average*
unter diesen Umständen	*in these circumstances*
unter anderem	*among other things*
heute vor einer Woche	*a week ago today*

A⟩⟩ Here is a list of places where you might go at lunchtime. In each case, start off the sentence with 'Ich gehe in ...'. You are talking about movement to a place, so you will need the accusative.

1 das Esszimmer
2 der Garten
3 das Gasthaus
4 die Gaststätte
5 das Hotel
6 die Konditorei
7 die Küche
8 das Restaurant
9 der Speisesaal
10 die Wirtschaft

B⟩⟩ Now use the same list of places, but start the sentence differently. Begin with 'Ich esse in ... '. This time, no movement is implied, so you will need the dative.

C⟩⟩ The following statements indicate where things belong in a room. In each case, say that you will put them there.

e.g. Die Blumen stehen auf dem Tisch.
Ich stelle die Blumen auf den Tisch.

You will need the verbs **stellen**, **hängen**, **legen** and **werfen**.

1 Das Bild hängt an der Wand.
2 Die Kissen liegen auf dem Sofa.
3 Der Papierkorb steht unter dem Tisch.
4 Der Computer steht auf dem Regal.
5 Der Wecker steht auf dem Schränkchen.
6 Der Stuhl steht in dem Garten.
7 Der Mantel hängt an der Tür.
8 Der CD-Spieler steht auf dem Schränkchen.
9 Der Abfall liegt auf dem Boden.

D⟩⟩ Answer the following questions based on the English clues:

1 Wo steht Roswithas Computer? (*on the shelf*)
2 Wohin stellt Roswitha ihren Computer? (*on the shelf*)
3 Wo hängen ihre Kleider (*in the wardrobe*)
4 Wohin hängt sie ihre Kleider? (*in the wardrobe*)
5 Wo steht die Blumenvase? (*on the table*)
6 Wohin stellt Roswitha die Blumenvase? (*on the table*))
7 Wohin geht Roswitha gern? (*to the Grünburg Park*)
8 Wo sitzt sie gern? (*in the Grünburg Park*)
9 Wo hängt der Poster? (*on the wall*)
10 Wohin hängt Roswitha den Poster? (*on the wall*)
11 Wohin stellt sie den Koffer? (*under the bed*)
12 Wo liegt der Koffer? (*under the bed*)
13 Wo arbeitet ihr Freund? (*in an office*)
14 Wohin geht er? (*to the office*)

Der Abfall liegt auf dem Boden

5.5 Prepositions with genitive

während des Semesters   während der Semesterferien

○ A small number of prepositions take the genitive. The most common of these are:

(an)statt
statt eines Radios
instead of a radio

trotz
trotz des Regens
despite the rain

während
während des Semesters
during the term

wegen
wegen des Regens
because of the rain

In colloquial German nowadays the dative is frequently used. But the genitive is still regarded as 'correct'.

A》 Combine two sentences into one:

e.g. Es regnet. Aber wir fahren in den Taunus.
Trotz des Regens fahren wir in den Taunus.

1   Es gibt einen Streik. Wir können nicht kommen.
Wegen ... können wir nicht kommen.
2   Ich habe Mittagspause. Ich gehe einkaufen.
Während ... gehe ich einkaufen.
3   Die Nachbarn machen viel Lärm. Ich kann nicht schlafen.
Wegen ... kann ich nicht schlafen.
4   Susan hat keine Zeit, Briefe zu schreiben. Sie schickt ihren Eltern eine Postkarte.
Statt ... schickt sie eine Postkarte.

Summary of prepositions and cases

Accusative	Accusative or Dative	Dative	Genitive
bis	an	aus	statt
durch	auf	außer	trotz
für	entlang	bei	während
gegen	hinter	gegenüber	wegen
ohne	in	mit	
um	neben	nach	
	über	seit	
	unter	von	
	vor	zu	
	zwischen		

B⟩⟩ In the following passage, you will encounter several of the prepositions you have met so far. Can you remember which case goes with which?

Dieter, ein Freund von Roswitha, studiert auch in Frankfurt. Er erzählt: „Ich bekomme mein Stipendium von d___ (1) Deutschen Forschungsgemeinschaft. Ich arbeite an mein___ (2) Dissertation. Von mein___ (3) Eltern bekomme ich kein Geld, sie haben selbst nicht genug. Ich bin seit fünf Monat___ (4) in Frankfurt. Seit einig___ (5) Woche___ (6) wohne ich mit ein___ (7) Freund bei ein___ (8) alten Dame. Wir haben eine gemeinsame Küche und ein gemeinsames Bad. In d___ (9) Küche haben wir einen Herd, einen Kühlschrank und einen Schrank für unser___ (10) Geschirr. In d___ (11) Wohnzimmer steht d___ (12) Fernseher. Abends sitzen wir dort oft zusammen und sehen eine Fernsehsendung. Aber während d___ (13) Semester___ (14) studiert jeder in sein___ (15) Zimmer. Aus mein___ (16) Fenster kann ich das Haus von mein___ (17) Freundin sehen. Meine Kleider hänge ich in d___ (18) Kleiderschrank. Ordentlich ist es nicht in mein___ (19) Zimmer, weil ich nicht genug Platz habe."

5.6 Preposition and article combined

im Norden	vom Sokrates-Programm	zur Haltestelle

○ There are a number of stock combinations of preposition and article into a single word. The most important are:

an das	→	ans	unter das	→	unters
an dem	→	am	unter dem	→	unterm
auf das	→	aufs	von dem	→	vom
bei dem	→	beim	vor das	→	vors
für das	→	fürs	vor dem	→	vorm
in das	→	ins	zu dem	→	zum
in dem	→	im	zu der	→	zur

These abbreviations are not always used. You can say:

Ich gehe zur Post.
I am going to the Post Office (it doesn't matter which one).

but to stress a particular place or thing, you use the fuller form:

Ich gehe zu der Post am Marktplatz.
I am going to the Post Office on the Market Square.

>> Make the following sentences sound more natural by combining the preposition and article:

e.g. Wir gehen sehr oft in das Kino.
Wir gehen sehr oft ins Kino.

1   Susans Bruder geht auf das Gymnasium.
2   Roswitha stellt viele Sachen unter das Bett.
3   Ich laufe schnell zu der Post und kaufe Briefmarken.
4   Ich gehe zu dem Bahnhof und kaufe meine Fahrkarte.
5   In dem Theater spielt morgen Abend Shakespeares „Hamlet".

5.7 *hin* and *her, hier, da* and *dort*

Wo stellst du deinen Computer hin?	Sie ruft mich rüber.
Mal bin ich hier, mal bin ich dort.	Schon bin ich da.
Was ich suche, ist nicht da.	Ich kann hinfahren.

O The two short adverbs **hin** and **her** are frequently used in German to indicate movement away from (**hin**) or towards (**her**) the subject. There is no equivalent in English, so frequently it is not possible to convey the same sense in translation.

> Meine Freunde gehen heute abend ins Kino. Ich gehe auch hin.
> *My friends are going to the cinema this evening. I'm going (there) too.*

> Wo stellst du deinen Computer hin, wenn du mit der Arbeit fertig bist?
> *Where do you put your computer when you have finished working?*

Frequently, **hin** and **her** are combined with prepositions, again with the meaning of movement away or towards.

> Roswitha geht in das Haus **hinein**.
> Roswitha kommt aus dem Garten **herein**.

The most important such combinations are:

hinauf	herauf
hinaus	heraus
hinein	herein
hinüber	herüber
hinunter	herunter

In spoken German, these are frequently shortened to:

rauf raus rein rüber runter

regardless of whether it should be **hin** or **her**!

e.g. Sie ruft mich schon mal rüber auf eine Tasse Kaffee.
She sometimes asks me over for a cup of coffee.

○ **hin** and **her** also combine to form (separable) verbs, e.g. **hinfahren, herkommen.** Sometimes they are used together, as in:

> ein ewiges Hin- und Herfahren
> a *continuous to-ing and fro-ing*

○ The words **hier, da** and **dort** can cause problems since their meaning does not correspond exactly with *here* and *there*.

hier can only mean *here*

dort can only mean *there*

da is less emphatic and can in fact mean both *here* and *there*.

e.g. Tut mir leid, Herr Müller ist im Moment nicht da.
I'm sorry, Mr Müller isn't here at present.

A〉〉 In the following anecdote, insert 'hin' or 'her as appropriate:

Roswitha steht vor ihrem Fenster und schaut (**1**) ___aus. Draußen sieht sie Dieter und ruft: „Dieter, komm doch mal auf eine Tasse Kaffee (**2**)___ ein!". Dieter geht die Treppe (**3**) ___auf und klopft an die Tür. Roswitha ruft von innen: „Komm schon (**4**) ___ein, die Tür ist nicht abgeschlossen!", und Dieter öffnet die Tür. Weil das Wetter so schön ist, beschließen die beiden, eine kurze Radtour durch den Park zu machen. Sie laufen die Treppe (**5**) ___unter. Roswitha holt ihr Fahrrad aus dem Keller. Beide fahren zusammen durch die Stadt, bis sie (**6**) ___aus aufs Land kommen.

B〉〉 Translate the following into German. Note that in some of them you will have a choice of 'hier' or 'da', in others 'dort' or 'da'.

1   Where is the book? There, on the table.
2   Is Roswitha there? Yes, she's here.
3   Here I am!
4   Where is the printer? Here, under the table.

5.8 Compounds with *da-*

---

darauf   **daneben**   **darunter**

○ A number of prepositions are only followed by a pronoun when the pronoun refers to a person rather than a thing. For things, a compound with **da-** is used instead.

> *with him* is **mit ihm**   *with it* is **damit**
> *for her* is **für sie**   *for it* is **dafür**
> *in front of him* is **vor ihm**   *in front of it* is **davor**

The most important **da-** compounds are:

dabei   daneben
dadurch   davon
dafür   davor
dagegen   dazu
dahinter   dazwischen
danach

Most of these have several meanings; look them up in a dictionary.

If the preposition starts with a vowel, an additional **r** is inserted to make the compound pronounceable:

daran   darin
darauf   darüber
daraus   darunter

The equivalent question forms are constructed with **wo-** or **wor-**:

womit?   *with what?*
wovon?   *of what?*
worüber?   *about what?*

○ Where the pronoun following the preposition refers to a person, you use the pronoun as usual.

> Hier kommt Dieter. Ich fahre mit ihm in die Stadt.
> *Here comes Dieter. I am going with him into the town.*

>> Shorten the following sentences by substituting the words in italics with either a pronoun or a 'da-' compound:

1   Ich fahre gerne mit *dem Fahrrad* in die Stadt.
2   Ich wohne bei *meiner Oma.*
3   Ich lege die Bücher auf *den Schreibtisch.*
4   Neben *dem Schreibtisch* steht der Papierkorb.
5   Ich weiß nichts von *diesem Vorschlag.*
6   Ich habe einen Brief von *Dieter.*

5.9 Verb + preposition

Sie erzählt Susan von ihrem Zimmer.

○   There are a large number of fixed combinations of verb and preposition which have become firmly established in German. Among the most important, and therefore worth learning, are shown below:

an	denken an (+acc.)	*to think of*
	sich erinnern an (+acc.)	*to remember*
	sich gewöhnen an (+acc.)	*to get used to*
	glauben an (+acc.)	*to believe in*
auf	antworten auf (+acc.)	*to answer*
	warten auf (+acc.)	*to wait for*
	sich freuen auf (+acc.)	*to look forward to*
aus	bestehen aus (+dat.)	*to consist of*
für	sorgen für (+acc.)	*to take care of*
	sich interessieren für (+acc.)	*to be interested in*
in	sich verlieben in (+acc.)	*to fall in love with*
mit	sprechen mit (+dat.)	*to speak to*

über	sich freuen über (+acc.)	*to be pleased about*
um	sich bewerben um (+acc.) bitten um (+acc.)	*to apply for* *to ask for*
von	sich verabschieden von (+dat.)	*to say goodbye to*

A》 Complete the following sentences with the appropriate prepositions and endings:

1   Susan verabschiedet sich ___ d___ Oma.
2   Dieter gewöhnt sich ___ d___ Leben in Frankfurt.
3   Roswitha freut sich ___ d___ Semesterferien.
4   Hans wartet an der Bushaltestelle ___ sein___ Freundin.
5   Susan spricht ___ ein___ Studentin.
6   Susan denkt oft ___ ihr___ Eltern in England.
7   Sie antwortet sofort ___ d___ Brief von ihren Eltern.
8   Dieter bewirbt sich ___ ein___ Stelle in Frankfurt.
9   Susan interessiert sich ___ d___ Leben in Deutschland.
10   Roswitha bittet ihren Vater ___ Geld.
11   Ich freue mich sehr ___ d___ Geschenk.

B》 Recapping various prepositions from this chapter, can you complete the following? It is Susan talking about a letter she is writing.

Ich schreibe einen Brief ___ **(1)** meine Freundin. Ich erzähle ihr ___ **(2)** meinem Besuch ___ **(3)** Deutschland. ___**(4)** meines Urlaubs habe ich viel ___ **(5)** Deutschland gesehen. Alle waren sehr nett ___ **(6)** mir und ich war ___ **(7)** vielen Familien eingeladen. Ich bin oft ___ **(8)** Kino gegangen, war auch ___ **(9)** Theater und ___ **(10)** der Oper. Einmal sind wir sogar ___ **(11)** Bad Dürkheim ___ **(12)** Wurstmarkt gefahren.

6 Knowing what to say next

Die Kölner feiern Karneval

Andere Länder, andere Sitten

Susan unterhält sich mit Hans, Dieter und Roswitha über
Sitten und Gebräuche in England und Deutschland

Hans	Susan, du bist jetzt schon **einige Wochen hier in Deutschland. Findest du das Leben hier anders** als in England?	6.4 6.5
Susan	**Große Unterschiede gibt es nicht**, aber ihr steht früher auf. Das Essen ist auch etwas anders.	6.1 / 6.6
Dieter	Diese Unterschiede bestehen auch zwischen Sachsen und Hessen. Die Sachsen **stehen** noch früher **auf** und essen auch andere Spezialitäten.	6.3

Hans	**Regionale Spezialitäten gibt es in ganz Deutschland.** In Thüringen isst man Thüringer Klöße, in Frankfurt Frankfurter Würstchen, in Bayern Weißwürste.	6.1
Dieter	Aber es gibt noch mehr Unterschiede. Die Norddeutschen sind reserviert und die Bayern ..., **aber das weißt du bestimmt schon**.	6.1
Hans	Einen wichtigen Unterschied kann ich dir mit der Fastnacht erklären. **Hier in Frankfurt und in Mainz feiern wir Fastnacht,** die Kölner feiern Karneval und die Münchner den Fasching. In der Faschingszeit gibt es auch Sonderzüge. Nach Düsseldorf und Köln fährt der Sonderzug „Pappnase" **morgens um 6 Uhr von Hamburg ins Rheinland**. Abends um 18 Uhr kann man dann mit demselben Zug wieder **zurückfahren**.	6.1 6.4 6.3
Dieter	Das reicht über Sitten und Gebräuche! Kannst du mir bitte die Schokolade **herüberreichen**?	6.3
Susan	Die Schokolade kannst du haben. Aber **iss nicht so viel**, sonst wirst du zu dick.	6.6
Dieter	Ich und zunehmen? Kein Problem! **Erstens nehme ich nicht zu** und zweitens **fahre** ich viel **Rad** und **gehe viel spazieren**. Dabei nimmt man ab.	6.6 6.3 6.2
Hans	Ja, ja. Darf ich das Thema wechseln? Susan, **könntest du** mir mal ein Loch in meiner Hosentasche flicken?	6.5
Susan	Das sind aber Sitten hier bei euch in Deutschland! In England machen das die Männer selbst.	
Roswitha	Und in Deutschland auch! **Hans hat nur eine Dumme gesucht**.	6.2
Dieter	Und nächstens repariert ihr euch auch eure Autos selbst und macht eure Türen selbst auf und bezahlt euer Bier	
Roswitha	**Tun wir ja schon!**	6.1

6.1 Main verb position

> Große Unterschiede gibt es nicht.
> Regionale Spezialitäten gibt es in ganz Deutschland.
> Aber das weißt du bestimmt schon.
> Tun wir ja schon!
> Hier in Frankfurt und in Mainz feiern wir Fastnacht.

○ In an English sentence, the subject of the action always precedes the verb. This is the only means we have of showing which is the subject. For example, the difference in meaning between:

> *The dog bites the man.*
> and   *The man bites the dog.*

is shown only by the position of *man* and *dog* in the sentence.

In German whether you say

> Der Hund beißt den Mann.
> OR   Den Mann beißt der Hund.

it is still the dog biting the man, because **der Hund** is nominative and can only be the subject, whereas **den Mann** is accusative and can only be the object, no matter where in the sentence they occur.

The most important word order rule in German is that only one element can come before the main verb. The verb is accordingly the *second idea* in the sentence.

> Ich **fahre** morgen nach Köln.
> Nach Köln **fahre** ich morgen.
> Morgen **fahre** ich nach Köln.

(The only exception is in questions and requests; see section 6.5.)

In English, any number of elements can precede the verb, provided that the subject is one of them. We can say:

> *Having packed my luggage already, early tomorrow morning*
> *and without time to say goodbye, I shall be leaving for Cologne.*

In this example, *I* is the subject and *shall be leaving* is the verb. You will see that there are three quite large chunks of language before either of them.

In German, you cannot do this. So when speaking or writing German, you must remember to make the verb the second element.

○ In the majority of German sentences, the first element is indeed the subject. But this is by no means always the case. Since a sentence is usually part of a longer narrative or a dialogue, you can use the first element to link the sentence to what has just been said.

Look at these examples from our text:

> Große Unterschiede **gibt** *es* nicht.
> Regionale Spezialitäten **gibt** *es* in ganz Deutschland.
> Hier in Frankfurt und Mainz **feiern** *wir* Fastnacht.

The verb is shown in bold print, and the subject in italics. In the first two cases, if you look back at the dialogue, you will see that the speaker is picking up something that someone else has just said. The third example is a development of what Hans is explaining; it also shows how the first element can be far more than one word, but it must be a single concept or idea.

○ Note that there are a few short words which can introduce a sentence without themselves being the first element. These include:

> **ja**
> **nein**
> **ach**
> **aber**
> **und**

as in our example:

> Aber das **weißt** *du* bestimmt schon.

where **aber** merely introduces the sentence and **das** is the first element.

○ Occasionally, the first element is implied or omitted, as in:

> **Tun** *wir* ja schon!

which is a shortened version of:

> Das **tun** *wir* ja schon!

A〉〉 Rewrite the following sentences starting with the phrase in italics. Remember that the verb must come next!

1 Es gibt *in ganz Deutschland* regionale Spezialitäten.
2 Ich repariere *mein Auto* selbst.
3 Ich flicke *meine Hosentasche* selbst.
4 Schokolade esse ich *am liebsten*.
5 Hans fährt *jeden Morgen* mit seinem Auto von Usingen nach Frankfurt zur Arbeit.

How many other ways are there of starting the same sentences?

B〉〉 The following statements all start with 'man'. As such, they are rather boring. Make them into a more interesting sequence by starting each sentence with the region you are referring to.

e.g. Man isst Thüringer Klöße in Thüringen.
In Thüringen isst man Thüringer Klöße.

1 Man feiert Karneval in Köln.
2 Man feiert Fastnacht in Mainz.
3 Man feiert Fasching in München.
4 Man feiert Fasnet im Dreiländereck zwischen Freiburg, Basel und Straßburg.

C〉〉 A computer technician is explaining her hard working day. We have listed the statements, together with some adverbs which she might use to link them into a single narrative. Make up the complete narrative using the adverbs to start each new sentence.

e.g. morgens   Das harte Leben fängt schon an.
Morgens fängt das harte Leben schon an.

1	oft	Ich bekomme einen Brief mit einem Problem.
2	meistens	Das ist nicht so einfach.
3	zwischendurch	Das Telefon klingelt.
4	dann	Ich unterbreche die Arbeit.
5	danach	Ich beginne wieder von Anfang an.
6	außerdem	Es gibt noch viele Probleme vom Vortag.
7	am besten	Ich lege alle Probleme in den Aktenschrank.
8	dann	Ich trinke eine Tasse Kaffee.

6.2 Second verb position

> Ich gehe viel spazieren.
> Hans hat nur eine Dumme gesucht.

○ Frequently, the verb will consist of more than one word. This occurs, for example:

with two verbs combined	ich **gehe spazieren**
with modal verbs, e.g. *can, will*	ich **kann erzählen**
in the past tense	ich **habe gekauft**
in the future	ich **werde kaufen**
with separable verbs	ich **kaufe ein**

We shall deal with some of these in more detail later. For the time being, what we need to note is that in all these cases, the first part of the verb takes the second element position in the sentence (see section 6.1), but the second part of the verb goes at the end of the clause.

We can talk of the verb forming a bracket around the rest of the clause:

Ich **gehe** jeden Tag **spazieren**.
Sie **hat** heute in der Stadt Obst und Gemüse **gekauft**.
Susan **wird** am Samstag einen neuen Pullover **kaufen**.
In der Disko **lernt** Susan Hans **kennen**.
Hans **hat** nur eine Dumme **gesucht**.

○ But which part of the verb goes in which slot? The part which opens the bracket is always the ***finite verb***, that is the part which changes according to the subject. The part which goes in the closing bracket position is that part which never changes.

Ich **gehe** jeden Tag **spazieren**.
Er **geht** jeden Tag **spazieren**.
Wir **gehen** jeden Tag **spazieren**.

Ich **habe** heute in der Stadt Obst und Gemüse **gekauft**.
Er **hat** heute in der Stadt Obst und Gemüse **gekauft**.
Wir **haben** heute in der Stadt Obst und Gemüse **gekauft**.

A In the following sentences, place the two parts of the verb in the correct position.

1	(kann fahren)	Ich (*can go*) nächste Woche nach Frankfurt.
2	(habe gekauft)	Ich (*have bought*) eine neue Jacke.
3	(wird fahren)	Er (*will go*) morgen nach Bad Dürkheim.
4	(hat gekauft)	Roswitha (*has bought*) ein schönes Kostüm für die Fastnacht.
5	(lernt kennen)	Dieter (*gets to know*) Susan und Jane.
6	(kann erzählen)	Hans (*can tell*) sehr viel von der Fastnacht.
7	(muss kaufen)	Susan (*must buy*) eine neue Bluse.
8	(möchte besuchen)	Roswitha (*would like to visit*) ihre Familie in Alzey.
9	(kann flicken)	Susan (*can mend*) das Loch in der Hose.

B Here is a list of activities:

schwimmen gehen; reiten gehen; turnen gehen; essen gehen; spazieren gehen; Tennis spielen; Ski laufen.

Put them into the following sentences as appropriate:

1 Im Sommer _____ ich im See_____ .

2 Im Winter _____ ich gern _____ .

3 Meine Schwester _____ jeden Sonntag im Reitstadion _____ .

4 Wir _____ in ein sehr schönes Restaurant _____ .

5 Im Schwarzwald _____ ich gern _____ .

6 In der Turnhalle _____ ich ab und zu _____ .

7 Wir _____ auf dem Sportplatz gern _____ .

6.3 Compound verbs

Die Sachsen stehen noch früher auf.
Abends kann man mit demselben Zug zurückfahren.
Kannst du mir bitte die Schokolade herüberreichen?
und zweitens fahre ich viel Rad

○ Many verbs in German are formed by compounding a simple verb with a prefix.

e.g. from	**steigen**	*to climb*
you have:	**einsteigen**	*to get in/on*
	aussteigen	*to get out/off*
	umsteigen	*to change*

○ The prefix is usually a preposition, as in all the above examples. But it could also be:
- one of a limited range of adjectives or adverbs,

    e.g. **fernsehen** *to watch television*

- a noun, provided that the compound is almost always used as an infinitive,

    e.g. **bergsteigen** *to climb a mountain*
    sonnenbaden *to sunbathe*

- a prefix that cannot be used independently

    e.g. **verstehen** *to understand*

○ Prior to the spelling reform, German had far more compound verbs, because the range of prefixes was much wider. Since the reform, the verbs are now written as two words rather than as a compound.

e.g. Old	New
bekanntmachen, *to announce*	**bekannt machen**
radfahren *to cycle*	**Rad fahren**
spazierengehen *to fo for a walk*	**spazieren gehen**
kennenlernen *to get to know*	**kennen lernen**

If you are in doubt as to whether a combination of noun+verb, adjective+verb or adverb+verb should be written as separate words or as a compound, check in an up-to-date dictionary.

○ Some compound verbs are **separable**, others are **inseparable**. The inseparable ones are easy, because the compound verb behaves just like any other simple verb. For example, **unterschreiben** is an inseparable verb meaning *to sign*. You say simply:

> ich **unterschreibe** den Brief

OR if the inseparable verb is the second verb in a sentence:
> ich muss den Brief **unterschreiben.**

In the case of the separable verbs, however, where they are used as the only verb in the sentence, the prefix is detached from the stem and takes the second verb position at the end of the clause:

> Ich **steige** an der nächsten Haltestelle **um.**
> Wir **stehen** noch früher **auf.**

But when the compound verb is itself the second part of a verbal element, i.e. when the whole of it takes the second verb position at the end, the prefix remains joined:

> Ich **kann** an der nächsten Haltestelle **umsteigen.**
> Wir **müssen** noch früher **aufstehen.**
> Abends **kann** man mit demselben Zug **zurückfahren.**

The following prefixes are always **inseparable:**

be-	**emp-**	**ent-**	**er-**
ge-	**miss-**	**ver-**	**zer-**

e.g. **beginnen**   *to begin*
verkaufen   *to sell*
zerbrechen   *to smash*

The following are **separable** when the meaning is taken concretely, but **inseparable** when there is a more abstract meaning:

durch-	**hinter-**	**um-**
unter-	**über-**	**wider-**

e.g. **durchschauen** (sep.)   *to look through*
Tolles Mikroskop. Schau mal durch!

durchschauen (insep.)   *to see through*
Ich durchschaue immer deine Lügen.

übersetzen (sep.)   *to ferry across*
Er setzte die Passagiere nach Cuxhaven über.

übersetzen (insep.)   *to translate*
Er übersetzte den Brief.

All other prefixes are always **separable.**

e.g. **ankommen**   *to arrive*
    aufstehen   *to get up*
    einkaufen   *to go shopping*

Der Zug kommt um drei Uhr an.
Ich stehe um sieben Uhr auf.
Ich kaufe in der Stadt ein.

A》 Put the separable verbs 'fernsehen', 'aufstehen', 'ankommen', 'umsteigen' and 'mitfahren' in the right place in the following sentences. You will need to watch the ending on the verb part!

1 Susan _____ nach Bad Dürkheim _____ .

2 Abends _____ die Kinder _____ .

3 Wir _____ erst um 21 Uhr in Bad Dürkheim _____ .

4 In Sachsen _____ man sehr früh _____ .

5 In Frankfurt _____ man oft _____ .

B》 The following sentences all include compounds of 'schreiben'. How would you translate them into English?

1 Der Arzt verschreibt mir Tabletten.
2 Das ist kein Fehler, ich habe mich nur verschrieben.
3 Der Student schreibt die richtige Lösung von seinem Freund ab.
4 Der Abteilungsleiter unterschreibt den Brief.
5 Die Firma hat das neue Projekt ausgeschrieben.
6 Man hat uns neue Regeln vorgeschrieben.

C》 The following sentences all contain inseparable verbs. Put them into the correct form.

1 Hans, Dieter und Roswitha (*tell*) Susan von den Sitten und Gebräuchen in Deutschland.
2 Die Wissenschaftler (*discover*) immer mehr Probleme mit dem Treibhauseffekt. Manchmal (*misunderstand*) die Medien, was die Wissenschaftler sagen wollen.
3 Die vier Studenten (*try*) verschiedene regionale Spezialitäten.
4 Dieter (*recommends*) Thüringer Klöße.
5 Nach dem Essen (*visit*) Susan den Frankfurter Zoo.

D》 All the following were written as compounds prior to the spelling reform. Which should now be written as two words?

1	sitzenbleiben	5	vollstopfen
2	skifahren	6	vollenden
3	fallenlassen	7	schiefgehen
4	zurückgeben	8	wiedererkennen

6.4 Word order in the rest of the clause

einige Wochen hier in Deutschland
morgens um 6 Uhr von Hamburg ins Rheinland

There are also rules for determining the order of words within the bracket. For producing acceptable German sentences, the following guidelines will be sufficient:

○ If the subject was not the first element in the sentence, it will normally come immediately after the verb.

e.g. Morgen kommt **mein Freund** aus Frankfurt.
Tomorrow my friend from Frankfurt is coming.

Wahrscheinlich kommt **er** morgen.
He will probably come tomorrow.

○ A useful rule of thumb is **time-manner-place**. This is not 100% foolproof when analysing German sentences, but again a useful guide when you are speaking or writing German.

e.g. Ich fahre **morgen nach Frankfurt.**
I am going to Frankfurt tomorrow.

Susan fährt **nächste Woche mit dem Zug nach Bad Dürkheim.**
Susan is going by train to Bad Dürkheim next week.

○ The object of the verb is often delayed more than it would be in English.

e.g. Ich schreibe heute abend **einen Brief.**
I am going to write a letter this evening.

○ If there are two nouns, the accusative will come last:

Ich schenke meiner Oma **einen Schal.**

○ If there is a pronoun and a noun, the pronoun will come first:

Ich schenke **ihn** meiner Oma.

○ If there are two or more pronouns after the verb, they will come in the sequence **nominative-accusative-dative**:

Ich schenke **ihn ihr.**
Morgen schenke **ich ihn ihr.**

A》 Practise the time-manner-place sequence by inserting the phrase in brackets into each of the following sentences:

1 Ich fahre mit dem Auto zur Arbeit. (jeden Morgen um 7 Uhr)
2 Die Fastnacht feiert man in vielen Teilen Deutschlands. (jedes Jahr)
3 Hans frühstückt jeden Morgen zu Hause. (um 8 Uhr)
4 Roswitha geht jeden Morgen um 8 Uhr zur Universität. (zu Fuß)
5 Letztes Jahr bin ich mit dem Auto gefahren. (nach Deutschland)
6 Samstags fahre ich gern mit meiner Familie einkaufen. (nach Frankfurt)
7 Susan wird wieder nach Deutschland kommen. (nächstes Jahr)
8 Der Zug kommt auf Gleis 3 an. (pünktlich)
9 Nächste Woche fährt Dieter mit dem Auto auf Urlaub. (nach Italien)
10 Carlas Mutter fährt in die Stadt einkaufen. (schnell)

B》 The example below shows how pronouns can replace nouns. Apply the same pattern to each of the sentences which follow.

e.g. Hans erklärt Susan regionale Unterschiede.
Er erklärt Susan regionale Unterschiede.
Er erklärt ihr regionale Unterschiede.
Er erklärt sie Susan.
Er erklärt sie ihr.

1 Roswitha schenkt ihrer Mutter ein Buch.
2 Hans zeigt Susan die Stadt Frankfurt.
3 Susan schreibt ihren Eltern einen Brief.

6.5 **Questions and requests**

> Findest du das Leben anders?
> Könntest du mir ein Loch flicken?

○ Many questions in German are introduced by an **interrogative.** In these cases, the interrogative forms the initial element in the sentence and the rest proceeds as above:

> Susan kommt aus England.
> Wer kommt aus England?

> Heute fährt Hans nach Frankfurt.
> Wann fährt Hans nach Frankfurt?

> In Basel feiert man eine Woche später.
> Wo feiert man eine Woche später?

○ The most important interrogatives include:

wer?	*who?*
was?	*what?*
wo?	*where?*
wohin?	*where to?*
warum?	*why?*
wie?	*how?*
wie viel?	*how much?*
wie viele?	*how many?*
wie lange?	*how long?*
was für?	*what sort of?*

○ But if the question is one which can be answered with *yes* or *no*, no interrogative is needed. In this case, the verb begins the sentence:

> Kommt Susan aus England?
> Findest du das Leben anders?
> Könntest du mir ein Loch flicken?

English frequently cannot express this type of question so simply, with the result that the verb is often changed from a simple to a more complex form:

> Kommt Susan aus England?
> *Does Susan come from England?*

As a result, English learners of German are often tempted to translate word for word, when the simple German tense is all that is required:

Are you coming to the cinema tonight?
Kommst du heute abend ins Kino?

It is quite wrong to start the sentence with **Bist du ...?**

○ A similar sentence structure is used with the imperative (see section 1.5) to express commands and requests.

e.g. Gib mir bitte das Buch!
Fangen Sie sofort an!

A⟩⟩ Question the following statements by asking if each is really true.

e.g. In Hessen isst man am Faschingsdienstag Fastnachtskreppel.
Isst man in Hessen wirklich am Faschingsdienstag Fastnachtskreppel?

1 In England isst man am Fastnachtsdienstag Pfannkuchen.
2 In Thüringen isst man Thüringer Klöße.
3 Am Aschermittwoch ist die Fastnacht vorbei.
4 In Bayern trinkt man sehr viel Bier.
5 Der Sonderzug Pappnase fährt nur in der Karnevalszeit.
6 In Südamerika feiert man auch Karneval.
7 Am Rosenmontag gibt es in Köln einen großen Umzug.
8 Susan flickt das Loch in der Hosentasche.
9 Roswitha und Susan bezahlen ihr Bier selbst.
10 Dieter nimmt nicht zu.

B⟩⟩ Use 'wo', 'wohin', 'woher', 'wann', 'wer', 'was für', 'wie lange', 'wie', 'wie viel', 'wie viele', 'wen', 'wem' and 'warum' to ask the questions indicated:

Der Sonderzug „Pappnase" fährt morgens um 6.12 Uhr von Hamburg ins Rheinland

Ask (**1**) what the train is called, (**2**) what time it goes, (**3**) where it comes from, (**4**) where it goes to, and (**5**) what sort of train it is.

Hans führt jeden Tag eine Stunde seinen Hund im Park spazieren.

Ask (**6**) who takes the dog for a walk (**7**) when Hans takes his dog for a walk (**8**) where he takes the dog for a walk, and (**9**) for how long he takes his dog for a walk.

Tausende Menschen strömen jährlich ins Rheinland, um den Karnevalszug in Köln zu sehen.

> Ask (**10**) how many people come every year to the Rhineland to see the carnival procession; (**11**) what do the people want to see and (**12**) why do people come to the Rhineland.

In Aachen verleiht man dem witzigsten Politiker des Jahres „den Orden wider den tierischen Ernst".

> Ask (**13**) what is awarded (**14**) where and (**15**) to whom is it awarded.

Susan isst viel Schokolade, denn sie schmeckt ihr sehr gut.

> Ask (**16**) how much chocolate Susan eats and (**17**) why.

6.6 Negation

> Iss nicht zu viel!
> Erstens nehme ich nicht zu.
> Große Unterschiede gibt es nicht.

○ Knowing where to place the word **nicht** in a German sentence can be tricky, and generally only comes with experience. Sometimes it is easy, because you want to negate one particular word or phrase. You can say:

> Er kommt nicht heute, sondern morgen.
> *He isn't coming today, he's coming tomorrow.*

and the word *nicht* clearly goes before *heute*, because that is the word you are negating.

○ But what if you want to negate a whole sentence? In this case, German places the word **nicht** towards or at the end of the sentence.

> Große Unterschiede gibt es **nicht.**
> *There are no great differences.*

But any element which has to go to the end will go beyond the **nicht**. For example, anything taking the second verb position:

> Erstens nehme ich nicht **zu**.
> *For a start, I don't put on weight.*

(NOTE **zunehmen** *is* a separable verb and so the **zu** has to go to the end.)

In a request or advice, the **nicht** follows the verb

> Iss nicht zu viel
> *Don't eat too much.*

Other negatives (e.g. **niemals** *never;* **kaum** *hardly*) also take the same position in the clause.

○ Remember never to say **nicht ein**; always use **kein** (see section 3.1)

》 Contradict the following sentences by inserting **nicht** or **kein**:

1 Ich kaufe Schokolade.
2 Wir gehen morgen.
3 Wir gehen morgen in den Zoo.
4 Er wohnt in Frankfurt.
5 Er hat ein Auto.
6 Er fährt mit dem Auto in die Stadt.
7 Hier darf man parken.

Iss nicht zu viel!

7 Talking about the past

Jugend in der DDR

Der Sachse vom Campingplatz heißt Herr Schulz. Er ist
jetzt Mathematiklehrer an einer Schule in Frankfurt. Aber
er hat nicht immer dort gewohnt.   7.1

Roswitha	Man erkennt schon an Ihrer Stimme, dass Sie nicht aus Frankfurt kommen ...
Herr S.	Richtig, ich komme aus Leipzig. Deswegen diese andere Aussprache!
Roswitha	Und haben Sie auch in Leipzig studiert?

Herr S. Ich habe an der Humboldt-Universität in Ostberlin studiert und zwar Mathematik. Das war
noch zu DDR-Zeiten. **Ich habe Mathe studiert**,   7.1
weil man damals in diesem Studienfach am
wenigsten Politik spürte. **Ich hatte Glück** und   7.5
habe einen Studienplatz bekommen, obwohl   7.2
ich kein Parteimitglied war.

Roswitha Das war nicht automatisch nach dem Abitur?

Herr S. Keineswegs. Mein Freund war Sohn eines
Pfarrers. **Er hatte Abitur gemacht** und durfte   7.6
trotzdem nicht studieren.

Roswitha Also, **Sie sind** erst nach der Wende nach   7.3
Frankfurt **umgezogen**. Hat es Ihnen dann im
Westen gefallen?

Herr S. Ja, es hat mir schon gefallen und gefällt mir noch.
Ich habe eine gute Stelle. Aber alles war auf einmal
so teuer. Zum Beispiel **bin ich** früher in Berlin für   7.3
20 Pfennig überall **rumgefahren**, mit der U-Bahn,
mit der S-Bahn, mit dem Bus. Ich konnte das nach
der Wende nicht mehr. Und **wir hatten** damals   7.4
überhaupt mehr **Vergünstigungen**. Besonders
für die Jugend **hat man** in der alten DDR sehr
viel **getan**.   7.2

Roswitha	Wie meinen Sie das?	
Herr S.	Na ja, **das fing schon mit den Pionieren an**. Sie	7.4
	hatten immer etwas zu tun. **Es gab Zeltlager**	7.5
	und **man traf sich jede Woche**.	7.4
Roswitha	War das nicht sehr politisch?	
Herr S.	Schon, aber **als Kind hat man das nicht so**	7.1
	gemerkt. Man konnte mit den Freunden	
	etwas unternehmen. Es gab halt viel	
	Kameradschaft.	
Roswitha	**Sie sind also bei den Pionieren gewesen**?	7.3
Herr S.	Natürlich. Fast alle waren bei den Pionieren.	
Roswitha	Vermissen Sie überhaupt etwas von damals?	
Herr S.	Ja, die Kameradschaft von früher, die vermissen	
	viele meiner Generation. **Dann war die Mauer**	7.6
	auf einmal **gefallen**, das Leben wurde anders.	
	Es gab so viel zu tun, aber viele hatten kein	
	Geld, besonders die Arbeitslosen.	
Roswitha	Na ja, das stimmt schon. Aber wenn man	
	Geld hat, kann man es ausgeben, wie man will.	
Herr S.	Da haben Sie recht. Man kann auch sagen, was	
	man will. Früher konnte man das nicht. **Und**	
	man durfte nicht hinfahren, wohin man fahren	7.5
	wollte. Urlaub konnte man nur im Ostblock	
	machen.	
Roswitha	Aber jetzt sind die Zeiten vorbei.	
Herr S.	Schon. Aber dafür haben wir andere Probleme.	
	Früher haben wir keine Arbeitslosigkeit gekannt.	7.2
	Jetzt kennt jeder wenigstens einen, der arbeits-	
	lost ist. Und alles ist jetzt viel teurer.	
Roswitha	Ich denke, Sie sehnen sich ein wenig nach der	
	alten DDR!	
Herr S.	Das nicht. Aber einiges vermisse ich schon.	

7.1 Perfect tense – weak verbs

Er hat nicht immer dort gewohnt.
Ich habe Mathe studiert.
Als Kind hat man das nicht gemerkt.

○ The *perfect tense* is the form most commonly used in spoken German to talk about events which have already happened. As will be seen in more detail in section 7.5, it corresponds not only to the English perfect tense, but frequently to the English past tense as well.

Ich habe gemerkt.	*I have noticed; I noticed.*
Ich habe nicht gemerkt.	*I haven't noticed; I didn't notice.*

○ The perfect tense consists of two parts, the auxiliary **haben** or **sein** and the *past participle*. In this section and in section 7.2, we are only concerned with verbs which form their perfect tense with **haben**. We shall consider in section 7.3 those which form the perfect with **sein**.

For the majority of verbs, the past participle is formed by adding the prefix **ge-** and the suffix **-t** to the stem.

kaufen ich habe **ge**kauf**t** *I bought*
du hast **ge**kauf**t**
er/sie/es hat **ge**kauf**t**
wir/Sie/sie haben **ge**kauf**t**
ihr habt **ge**kauf**t**

merken ich habe **ge**merk**t**, du hast **ge**merk**t**, etc.
spielen ich habe **ge**spiel**t**, du hast **ge**spiel**t**, etc.

The form of **haben** takes the first verb position in its clause and the past participle the concluding verb position.

Er **hat** nicht immer dort **gewohnt.**
He has not always lived there.

○ All the verbs which add the suffix **-t** to form the past participle are called **weak verbs.** This is to distinguish them from the **strong verbs,** which are dealt with in section 7.2.

Some of them, however, do not require the prefix **ge-**. These are:

a) inseparable verbs (see section 6.3) which begin with:
   be-, ent-, emp-, er-, ge-, miss-, ver-, zer-.

   e.g. Ich habe erzählt. *I told.*
         Ich habe versucht. *I tried.*

b) verbs ending in **-ieren**

   e.g. Ich habe studiert. *I studied.*

Separable verbs (see section 6.3) insert the prefix **ge-** between the two components of the past participle.

e.g. Ich habe heute morgen *I went shopping this morning.*
      eingekauft.

Verbs whose stem ends in a **-d** or **-t** will require an additional **e** in the past participle (see section 1.3 for the present tense).

e.g. Ich habe gearbeitet. *I worked.*
      Wir haben im Meer gebadet. *We swam in the sea.*

》 The following are statements Herr Schulz might have made about himself when he was studying in Berlin. Now he is in Frankfurt looking back at those years. How would he express the same thoughts now?

e.g. Ich lebe billig.
      Ich habe billig gelebt.

1 Ich kaufe viele Bücher.
2 Ich studiere an der Humboldt-Universität.
3 Ich lerne Russisch.
4 Ich wohne in Berlin.
5 Ich habe ein Zimmer in einem Studentenwohnheim.
6 Ich räume das Zimmer jede Woche auf.
7 Die Fahrt mit der U-Bahn kostet 20 Pfennig.
8 Ich arbeite viel.
9 Ich rede nicht viel über Politik.

7.2 Perfect tense – strong and mixed verbs

> Man hat viel getan.
> Ich habe einen Studienplaz bekommen.
> Früher haben wir keine Arbeitslosigkeit gekannt.

○ In English, most verbs form their past participle with 'ed'.

e.g. live - lived
  dance - danced

But quite a large number take the ending 'n'.

e.g. give - given
  eat - eaten

or have no ending at all.

e.g. read - read

There is an even greater number of German verbs which do not form their past participle with **-t**. Instead, the past participle ends in **-en**, and there is frequently a vowel change as well.

e.g. Ich lese - Ich habe gelesen. *I read.*
  Ich trinke - Ich habe getrunken. *I drank.*

  Man tut - man hat getan. *One did.*
  Für die Jugend hat man sehr viel getan.
  A lot was done for young people.

These verbs are called irregular or **strong verbs.** You will find a list of the most important of them on pages 112-113 and a much longer list in any good dictionary.

○ Also included in German verb lists are a few verbs which can be regarded as **mixed**, in the sense that they form the past participle with **-t**, but with a vowel change.

e.g. Ich kenne - Ich habe gekannt. *I knew.*
  Ich denke - Ich habe gedacht. *I thought.*

○ Any compound forms with these verbs will form their past participle in the same way as the basic verb:

> basic verb **singen** *to sing*
> past participle **gesungen**
> compound verb **mitsingen** *to sing along*
> past participle **mitgesungen**

Like separable weak verbs, separable strong verbs insert the **-ge-** between the components:

> Ich spreche - Ich habe gesprochen. *I spoke.*
> Ich spreche nach - Ich habe nach**ge**sprochen. *I repeated.*

Inseparable strong verbs don't take the **ge-** at all:

> Ich verspreche - Ich habe versprochen. *I promised.*

○ Any verb which you cannot find in a dictionary strong verb list, and which is not a compound of a strong verb, you can assume to be weak!

>> Refer to the verb table on pages 112-113 and put the following into the perfect tense:

1 Susan wohnt zwei Wochen bei Carla.
2 Susan schreibt einen Brief an ihre Eltern.
3 Ich nehme die U-Bahn an der Hauptwache.
4 Die Oma in Alzey hebt trotz ihres Alters schwere Körbe.
5 Rüdiger mietet ein Zimmer in Frankfurt.
6 Carla findet ihren Flaschenöffner nicht.
7 Auf der Geburtstagsfeier trinken sie viel Wein.
8 Roswitha und Herr Schulz sprechen über die Vergangenheit.
9 Susan trifft Herrn Schulz auf dem Campingplatz.
10 Roswitha schläft lange.
11 Bei der Weinlese helfen die Familienmitglieder.
12 Der Film beginnt um acht Uhr.

7.3 Perfect tense with sein

> Ich bin rumgefahren.   Sie sind nach Frankfurt umgezogen.
> Sie sind bei den Pionieren gewesen?

○ In the King James Bible you will find some examples of English forming a perfect tense not with *to have* but with *to be*.

   e.g. I *am* come (rather than *I have come*).
       Babylon *is* fallen (rather than *Babylon has fallen*).

This use of *to be* has died out in English, but is still very alive in German. Indeed, many of the most common German verbs form their perfect tense with **sein** rather than **haben**.

○ The most important verbs in this group are:

a)   verbs of motion from one place to another
    kommen - Ich bin gekommen. *I came.*
    fahren - Ich bin gefahren. *I went.*
    fliegen - Ich bin geflogen. *I flew.*

b)   verbs which indicate a change of condition.
    werden - Ich bin geworden. *I became.*
    wachsen - Ich bin gewachsen. *I grew.*
    einschlafen - Ich bin eingeschlafen. *I fell asleep.*
    gebären - Ich bin geboren. *I was born.*

    and also:
    sein - Ich bin gewesen. *I was.*
    bleiben - Ich bin geblieben. *I stayed.*

In a dictionary you will find these verbs marked 'with **sein**' in the main entry and again if they are included in a strong/irregular verb list.

A》 In the following examples, translate into German the verb shown in English. In all cases, the first part of the verb will be a form of 'sein'.

1   Susan ___ nach Frankfurt _____. (*drove*)
2   Susan ___ mit Hans ins Kino _____. (*went*)
3   Rüdiger ___ sehr fleißig _____. (*was*)

4 Roswitha ___ um sieben Uhr _____. (*got up*)
5 Der Bus ___ um 17 Uhr am Hauptbahnhof _____. (*arrived*)
6 Gestern abend ___ ich zu Hause _____.(*stayed*)
7 Herr Schulz ___ nach der Wende nach Frankfurt _____. (*came*)
8 Ich ___ nicht lange in der Disko _____. (*stayed*)

B》 The following examples have the second part of the verb
completed. But is the first part a form of 'sein' or 'haben'?

1 Susan _____ auf der Geburtstagsfeier viel Wein getrunken.
2 Susan _____ nach Deutschland gefahren.
3 Hans _____ einen Opel gekauft.
4 Ich _____ einen Fehler gemacht.
5 Der Chef _____ von London nach Frankfurt geflogen.
6 Herr Schulz _____ nach der Wende nicht lange in Berlin
   geblieben.
7 Auf der Geburtstagsfeier _____ Hans mit Susan getanzt.
8 Hans _____ noch nie in England gewesen.
9 Aber er _____ einmal nach Amerika geflogen.
10 Susan _____ schon als Baby schwimmen gelernt.

C》 Roswitha tells Dieter about environmental problems and lists a few
that have occured in the past. Complete the text. As a help, we
have indicated with an asterisk the verbs which take 'sein'.

Von Tschernobyl _____ du bestimmt _____ (hören). Aber kurz
darauf _____ in einem Chemiewerk in der Schweiz ein Feuer
_____ (*ausbrechen). Davon _____ man damals viel in den
Zeitungen _____ (lesen)? Viele chemische Giftstoffe _____ in den
Rhein _____ (*kommen). Viele Fische _____ (*sterben).
Man _____ die toten Fische aus dem Rhein _____ (fischen). Alle
_____ sich fürchterlich über das Unglück _____ (aufregen). Die
Firma _____ man später _____ (freisprechen). Kurz darauf _____
ein anderes Unglück am Main _____ (*passieren). Wieder _____
viele Giftstoffe in den Rhein _____ (*fließen). In Spanien _____
der Inhalt eines mit Schwermetallen verschmutzten Sammelbeckens
_____ (*auslaufen) und _____ das Naturschutzgebiet Doñana
_____ (vergiften). Das gleiche _____ in Rumänien _____
(*geschehen). Das Unglück in Tschernobyl _____ vor vielen Jahren
_____ (*geschehen) und das Gebiet ist heute noch radioaktiv
verseucht, der Rhein _____ sich zum Teil _____ (erneuern) und

selbst die Ölverschmutzung an der Atlantikküste _____ allmählich
_____ (*verschwinden). Aber wie lange können wir die Umwelt
ohne nachhaltige Folgen für Menschen, Tiere und Pflanzen
verschmutzen?

7.4 Simple past tense

> Wir hatten Vergünstigungen.   Man traf sich jede Woche.
> Das fing schon mit den Pionieren an.

○ There is another way of expressing the past in German, which is to
use the **simple past tense**. For historical reasons, this is sometimes
called the imperfect, but this name bears no relationship to its use
in German and can be confusing. So we shall follow the practice of
modern grammars and call it the simple past. It is a tense primarily
used in the written rather than the spoken language (but for more
details of usage, see section 7.5).

○ Weak verbs form their simple past by adding **-te** to the stem.

e.g. kaufen   ich kauf**te**   *I bought*
              du kauf**test**
              er/sie/es kauf**te**
              wir/Sie/sie kauf**ten**
              ihr kauf**tet**

○ Strong verbs form the simple past mainly through a change of vowel.

e.g. sehen   ich **sah**   *I saw*
              du **sahst**
              er/sie/es **sah**
              wir/Sie/sie **sahen**
              ihr **saht**

       treffen   ich **traf**   *I met*
              Man **traf** sich jede Woche.
              We met every week.

In both weak and strong verbs, note that the 3rd person
(**er/sie/es**) form is the same as the **ich** form. In the case of strong
verbs, note also that there is no **-e** ending for the 1st/3rd person;
both end in the stem consonant.

◉ Mixed verbs both change the vowel and add **-te:**

> Ich bringe   Ich **brachte**   *I brought*

Verbs with a stem ending in **-d** or **-t** add an additional **-e** :

> Ich arbeite   Ich arbei**tete**   *I worked*

sein and **haben** both have irregular forms:

> Ich habe   Ich **hatte**   *I had*
> Ich bin   Ich **war**   *I was*

> Wir hatten Vergünstigungen.
> *We had discounts.*

In the case of separable verbs, the simple past verb takes the initial verb position and the prefix the final verb position:

> Das **fing** bei den Pionieren **an.**
> *It began with the Pioneers (junior branch of youth movement).*

A⟩⟩ Take the first two exercises from section 7.3 and write out the sentences again in the simple past form.

B⟩⟩ Winter can sometimes kick back very late. Some years ago, there was a sudden return of winter at the end of April. The following is a shortened version of a report which appeared in a Cologne newspaper. All the verbs are given in the infinitive; can you restore the original simple past forms?

Wer gestern aus dem Fenster (**1** schauen), (**2** können) am Wetter irre werden; Schnee, Regen, dann wieder Sonnenschein. Drei Tage vor dem 1. Mai (**3** zurückkommen) der Winter noch einmal. Selbst im Rheinland (**4** sinken) die Temperaturen wieder unter den Gefrierpunkt.

Allein die Autobahnwache Hagen (**5** registrieren) innerhalb weniger Stunden elf typische Winter-Unfälle. München (**6** versinken) in dichtem Schneetreiben.

Auch in England (**7** geben) es zum Teil heftige Schneefälle. Im Schneesturm (**8** stürzen) eine Privatmaschine nördlich von London ab. Die vier Insassen aus Holland (**9** kommen) ums Leben. Südlich von Plymouth (**10** sinken) ein Fischkutter; ein Flugzeugträger (**11** retten) die fünfköpfige Besatzung.

Past tense forms in German: verbs worth learning

Infinitive	Meaning	Simple past	Perfect
Strong verbs			
ei-ie-i/ie			
bleiben	*to stay*	ich blieb	ich bin geblieben
reiten	*to ride*	ich ritt	ich bin geritten
schneiden	*to cut*	ich schnitt	ich habe geschnitten
schreiben	*to write*	ich schrieb	ich habe geschrieben
steigen	*to climb*	ich stieg	ich bin gestiegen
e/ie/-o-o			
bieten	*to offer*	ich bot	ich habe geboten
heben	*to lift*	ich hob	ich habe gehoben
schließen	*to shut*	ich schloss	ich habe geschlossen
verlieren	*to lose*	ich verlor	ich habe verloren
ziehen	*to pull*	ich zog	ich habe gezogen
i-a-u			
finden	*to find*	ich fand	ich habe gefunden
singen	*to sing*	ich sang	ich habe gesungen
springen	*to jump*	ich sprang	ich bin gesprungen
trinken	*to drink*	ich trank	ich habe getrunken
e/i/o-a-o			
beginnen	*to begin*	ich begann	ich habe begonnen
brechen	*to break*	ich brach	ich habe gebrochen
gewinnen	*to win*	ich gewann	ich habe gewonnen
helfen	*to help*	ich half	ich habe geholfen
kommen	*to come*	ich kam	ich bin gekommen
nehmen	*to take*	ich nahm	ich habe genommen
sprechen	*to speak*	ich sprach	ich habe gesprochen
sterben	*to die*	ich starb	ich bin gestorben
treffen	*to meet*	ich traf	ich habe getroffen
werfen	*to throw*	ich warf	ich habe geworfen

Infinitive	Meaning	Simple past	Perfect
e/i/ie-a—e			
bitten	*to ask for*	ich bat	ich habe gebeten
essen	*to eat*	ich aß	ich habe gegessen
geben	*to give*	ich gab	ich habe gegeben
lesen	*to read*	ich las	ich habe gelesen
liegen	*to lie*	ich lag	ich habe gelegen
sehen	*to see*	ich sah	ich habe gesehen
sitzen	*to sit*	ich saß	ich habe gesessen
vergessen	*to forget*	ich vergaß	ich habe vergessen
a-u-a			
tragen	*to carry*	ich trug	ich habe getragen
fahren	*to drive*	ich fuhr	ich bin gefahren
schlagen	*to hit, beat*	ich schlug	ich habe geschlagen
a-i/ie-a			
fallen	*to fall*	ich fiel	ich bin gefallen
fangen	*to catch*	ich fing	ich habe gefangen
halten	*to hold*	ich hielt	ich habe gehalten
lassen	*to let*	ich ließ	ich habe gelassen
schlafen	*to sleep*	ich schlief	ich habe geschlafen
laufen	*to run*	ich lief	ich bin gelaufen
rufen	*to call*	ich rief	ich habe gerufen
tun	*to do*	ich tat	ich habe getan
gehen	*to go*	ich ging	ich bin gegangen
sein	*to be*	ich war	ich bin gewesen
stehen	*to stand*	ich stand	ich habe gestanden
werden	*to become*	ich wurde	ich bin geworden

Mixed verbs

bringen	*to bring*	ich brachte	ich habe gebracht
denken	*to think*	ich dachte	ich habe gedacht
kennen	*to know*	ich kannte	ich habe gekannt
wissen	*to know*	ich wusste	ich habe gewusst

7.5 Perfect or simple past?

> Es gab Zeltlager.   Ich hatte Glück.
> Man durfte nicht hinfahren, wohin man fahren wollte.

○ Compare the following sentences in English:

> *I applied for a job in Manchester.*
> *I have applied for a job in Manchester.*

The first can refer to any time in the past, and in fact is probably incomplete without some indication of when the application was made. The second sentence, on the other hand, indicates that the application is fairly recent and indeed, still current. The perfect tense in English can be said to have a reference to the present.

This is not the case in German, where the perfect tense is used in conversation to refer to any past event without necessarily applying to the present. Thus to an extent, the simple past and perfect tenses in German are interchangeable. However, there are differences in the *contexts* in which they are used.

First and foremost, the perfect is the tense of conversation, and the simple past the tense of written narrative. In spoken German you would probably say:

> Ich **habe** mich um eine Stelle in Manchester **beworben**.

regardless of how long ago this was. But in a written account of, say, what happened last year, you could write

> Ich **bewarb** mich um eine Stelle in Manchester.

○ The simple past is, however, used in conversation in the following circumstances:

a) with frequently used forms such as **ich war, ich hatte, ich sah, ich kam, ich ging, ich blieb, ich stand** and above all **es gab:**

> Es gab Zeltlager.   *There were camps.*
> Ich hatte Glück.   *I was lucky.*

b) with modal verbs **ich konnte, ich wollte, ich musste, ich durfte, ich sollte** (see section 8.1):

> Man durfte nicht hinfahren, wohin man fahren wollte.
> *You could not travel wherever you wished.*

c) to translate the English continuous past, *was ...ing:*

> Als ich studierte, gab es keine Stipendien.
> *When I was studying there were no* grants.

○ In written German, the perfect tense is used where the result of an action is still evident:

> Es hat in der Nacht geschneit.
> *It has snowed in the night.*

》 Herr Schulz is talking about his life in the old GDR:

So schlecht ist das Leben in der alten DDR auch nicht gewesen. Wir haben keine Arbeitslosen gekannt, wir haben billige Grundlebensmittel gehabt und man konnte billig mit dem Bus oder mit dem Zug fahren. Natürlich durften wir aber nicht reisen. Das haben wir alle sehr negativ empfunden. Bücher sind billig gewesen. Man konnte halt nur nicht alle Bücher kaufen. Ich habe Mathematik studiert, in naturwissenschaftlichen Fächern spürte man am wenigsten Politik. Wir haben natürlich auch politische Themen diskutiert, aber eben nicht so viel wie in den Geisteswissenschaften.

He is asked to write a short account for a local newspaper. What would he have written?

7.6 Looking even further back: the pluperfect

> Er hatte Abitur gemacht.   Dann war die Mauer gefallen.

○ Sometimes, you need to outline what *had* happened before another event took place. English does this with the past tense of *to have* and the past participle.

> *He had passed his A levels (and then went to university).*

In German, the same result is achieved in exactly the same way:

> Er **hatte** Abitur **gemacht.**

This is called the *pluperfect tense*. As with the perfect, the form of **haben** takes first verb position, and the past participle the concluding verb position.

Some more examples:

> Carla **hatte** Hans und Peter **eingeladen**. Also mussten die Mädchen das Abendessen vorbereiten.
> *Carla had invited Hans and Peter. So the girls had to prepare the evening meal.*

> Roswitha **hatte** einen Computer **gekauft**. Sie stellte ihn auf das Regal.
> *Roswitha had bought a computer. She put it on the shelf.*

○ If the verb is one which forms its perfect tense with **sein**, the pluperfect will be formed from the past tense of **sein**.

> Dann **war** die Mauer auf einmal **gefallen.**
> *Then suddenly the wall had come down.*

> Susan **war** noch nie auf einem Weingut **gewesen**.
> *Susan had never been to a vineyard before.*

○ The pluperfect is used in both spoken and written German.

○ In German (but not necessarily in English) the pluperfect indicates a completed action. If the action is still going on, the perfect or simple past is used, often with **seit**. Just as **seit** plus the present tense is used for an action begun in the past and continung to the present (see section 4.7), **seit** plus the simple past is used for a past activity still going on at the time the speaker is describing.

e.g. Susan war seit zwei Wochen in Deutschland. Dann ist sie nach Alzey gefahren.
Susan had been in Germany for two weeks. Then she went to Alzey (i.e. she was still in Germany).

Herr Schulz hatte sechs Jahre in Berlin studiert. Dann ist er nach Frankfurt umgezogen.
Herr Schulz had studied in Berlin for six years. Then he moved to Frankfurt (i.e. he had finished his studies).

A》 Make a list of things Herr Schulz *had done* before moving to Frankfurt.

    e.g. Mathematik studieren
            Er hatte Mathematik studiert.

  1   in Leipzig zur Schule gehen
  2   bei den Pionieren sein
  3   für die U-Bahn nur 20 Pfennige bezahlen
  4   oft mit der U-Bahn fahren
  5   überall herumfahren
  6   einen Studienplatz bekommen
  7   in Berlin studieren

B》 Read through again your answers to exercise B in section 4.5 (page 62). Now complete the following statements about events which *had happened* prior to the fall of the Wall.

    e.g. Ungarn _____ mit dem Abbau der Grenze _____.
            Ungarn hatte mit dem Abbau der Grenze begonnen.

  1   Ungarn _____ die Grenze nach Österreich _____
  2   In Leipzig _____ 20 000 Menschen _____.
  3   Eine große Militärparade _____ _____.
  4   Der Staatsratsvorsitzende _____ _____.
  5   Die größte Demonstration _____ am 4. November _____.
  6   Die Regierung _____ am 7. November _____.

8 Saying what you can, will or might do

Ich hätte keine Lust das ganze Leben lang zu studieren!

Berufswünsche

Die jungen Leute sitzen zusammen und diskutieren, was sie einmal werden wollen und ob sie das auch können.

Hans	**Was willst du denn einmal werden**, Dieter? **Man**	8.1
	kann doch nicht sein ganzes Leben studieren.	8.1
Dieter	Das kann man schon. **Lernen macht mir Spaß,**	8.2
	und **ich würde schon immer etwas Neues finden,**	8.4
	was mich interessiert.	
Hans	Ich hätte **keine Lust** das ganze Leben lang	8.2
	Mathematik zu studieren!	
Dieter	Das hat mein Bruder auch immer gesagt.	
	Er wollte immer etwas Praktisches machen.	8.1
	Deshalb hat er eine Lehre bei der Post gemacht.	
	Er musste auch lernen, aber halt nur Praktisches.	8.1
Roswitha	**Ich werde auch etwas Praktisches machen.**	8.3
	Vielleicht im Umweltschutz arbeiten. Da könnte	

	man etwas Positives leisten. **Und das wäre für unsere Zukunft auch sehr notwendig.**	8.4
Hans	Immer die Idealistin! **Ihr Studenten dürft euch nicht** so auf Idealberufe **versteifen.** Etwas Handfestes solltet ihr machen!	8.1
Roswitha	Du hast gut reden! Ein Computer ist auch nichts Handfestes. **Wenn ich nur wüsste,** wie man eine gute Stelle im Umweltschutz bekommt. **Es ist so schwer das Richtige zu finden. Ich wünschte, ich wäre schon fertig.** Im Moment überlege ich nur hin und her. **Meine Eltern hätten gerne,** dass ich zu Hause arbeite.	8.4 8.2 8.4 8.4
Hans	**Das wäre gut** — eine umweltbewusste Winzerin! Du könntest Verarbeitungsprozesse entwickeln, um den Abfall beim Keltern umweltfreundlich zu beseitigen! Ich habe neulich in einem Artikel gelesen: „**Könnte man die Abfälle umweltfreundlicher beseitigen,** so wäre dies ein großer Fortschritt."	8.4 8.5
Roswitha	Du **hast** auch nicht zu Hause **bleiben wollen.** Du bist nach Frankfurt gezogen. **Warum soll ich denn zu Hause bleiben?**	8.1 8.1
Hans	**Wenn du zu Hause bleibst, kommen wir dich besuchen.** Dann können wir wenigstens das Hauptprodukt der Weinernte umweltfreundlich beseitigen!	8.3/8.2

119

8.1 Modal verbs

Was willst du werden? Warum soll ich zu Hause bleiben?
Ihr dürft euch nicht versteifen.
Man kann nicht sein ganzes Leben studieren.
Er wollte immer etwas Praktisches machen.
Er musste auch lernen.
Du hast auch nicht zu Hause bleiben wollen.

○ A small number of verbs in German are known as **modal verbs**, because they are used in conjunction with a second verb to indicate a 'mood' of wanting, obligation, permission etc.

These verbs are:

können	**ich kann**	*I can, I am able to*
dürfen	**ich darf**	*I may, I am allowed to*
müssen	**ich muss**	*I must, I have to*
mögen	**ich mag**	*I like to, I may*
sollen	**ich soll**	*I am supposed to*
wollen	**ich will**	*I want to*

You will find a table showing the main parts of these verbs on the opposite page.

Note particularly the following:

a) In the present tense, the 1st (*I*) and 3rd (*he/she/it*) persons have the same form.

b) In the past tense, almost all the verbs have a vowel change.

○ The following notes will clarify the meanings and uses of each of the modals:

Ich kann is generally unproblematic since it is close to the English *I can*.

Ich darf means *I may* or *I am allowed to*. In the negative **ich darf nicht** is the equivalent of the English *I must not*.

Modal verbs: present and simple past

	können	dürfen	müssen	mögen	sollen	wollen
Present						
ich	kann	darf	muss	mag	soll	will
du	kannst	darfst	musst	magst	sollst	willst
er/sie/es	kann	darf	muss	mag	soll	will
wir/Sie/sie	können	dürfen	müssen	mögen	sollen	wollen
ihr	könnt	dürft	müsst	mögt	sollt	wollt
Simple past						
ich	konnte	durfte	musste	mochte	sollte	wollte
du	konntest	durftest	musstest	mochtest	solltest	wolltest
er/sie/es	konnte	durfte	musste	mochte	sollte	wollte
wir/Sie/sie	konnten	durften	mussten	mochten	sollten	wollten
ihr	konntet	durftet	musstet	mochtet	solltet	wolltet

Ich muss means *I must, I have to*. In the negative **ich muss nicht** simply implies *I do not have to* or *I need not*.

Ich mag is *I like*. It implies that you generally like doing something, as opposed to **ich möchte** which means *I would like*. It is the subjunctive form of **mögen** (see section 8.4).

> **ich möchte, du möchtest, er/sie/es möchte**
> **wir/Sie/sie möchten, ihr möchtet**

Ich mag Kaffee. *I like coffee.*
Ich möchte eine Tasse Kaffee. *I should like a cup of coffee (now).*

Ich soll implies *I shall* or *I am supposed to*.

Ich will is much stronger than **ich möchte** and is *I want to*. (For the future *I will* see section 8.3)

121

○ Where the modal is used in conjunction with a second verb, the modal takes the first verb position in the sentence; the second verb is used in the infinitive and takes the final verb position at the end.

> Ihr **dürft** euch nicht so **versteifen.**
> *You should not be so set on it.*

> Man **kann** nicht das ganze Leben lang **studieren.**
> *You can't go on studying all your life.*

In the perfect tense, the modal verbs have past participles **gekonnt, gedurft, gemusst, gemocht, gesollt, gewollt.** But these are not used if there is also another verb in the infinitive. Instead, you use the infinitive of both verbs:

> Ich habe es **gewollt.** *That's what I wanted.*
> Ich habe das Buch **lesen wollen.** *I wanted to read the book.*

So it is hardly surprising that with modals, the simple past tense is preferred!

> Ich **wollte** es.
> Ich **wollte** das Buch lesen.

A⟩⟩ Susan also talks about her future plans. In the following sentences, she makes various statements about what she must, can or would like to do. Clarify the meaning in each case by using the modal verb shown in brackets.

e.g. Ich lerne in der Schule sehr viel.   (müssen)
       Ich muss in der Schule sehr viel lernen.

1   Ich gehe nach York.   (wollen)
2   Dort studiert man auch Linguistik.   (können)
3   Ich arbeite auch mit Computern.   (sollen)
4   Ich lerne tüchtig.   (müssen)
5   Vielleicht arbeite ich auf dem Gebiet der   (können)
     Maschinenübersetzung.
6   Das ist sehr interessant.   (sollen)
7   Ich komme nächstes Jahr wieder nach Deutschland. (möchten)
8   Ich werde vielleicht Übersetzerin.   (können)
9   Ich arbeite für eine große Firma.   (möchten)
10 Ich arbeite auch freiberuflich.   (können)

B⟩⟩ The following sentences indicate situations which cannot be allowed to continue. In each case, use 'müssen' to indicate that things simply have to change.

    e.g. Ich möchte nicht in die Schule gehen.
          Ich muss aber in die Schule gehen.

1   Er lernt nicht gern.
2   Sie schreibt keine Briefe.
3   Wir verhalten uns nicht umweltfreundlich.
4   Du findest keine Stelle.
5   Ihr arbeitet nicht viel.
6   Sie machen sich keine Gedanken über die Zukunft.

C⟩⟩ Make the following sentences refer to a time in the past, by using the simple past.

    e.g. Ich muss viel arbeiten.
          Ich musste viel arbeiten.

1   Ich kann Deutschland besuchen.
2   Ich darf ins Kino gehen.
3   Ich soll mehr Grammatik lernen.
4   Er muss seine Hausaufgaben machen.
5   Sie will ein neues Kleid kaufen.

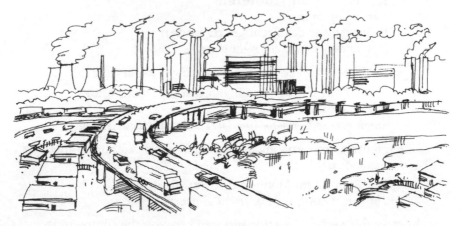

Wir verhalten uns nicht umweltfreundlich

8.2 Other uses of the infinitive

keine Lust Mathematik zu studieren
Lernen macht mir Spaß.
kommen wir dich besuchen
Es ist so schwer das Richtige zu finden.

● Besides the modal verbs, there are a number of other verbs which can be followed by a simple infinitive. These are:

bleiben	*to stay*	**lassen**	*to let*
gehen	*to go*		(see section 9.5)
helfen	*to help*	**lehren**	*to teach*
hören	*to hear*	**lernen**	*to learn*
kommen	*to come*	**sehen**	*to see*

e.g. Wir kommen dich besuchen.
We will come to visit you.
Ich lerne schwimmen.
I am learning to swim.

● After other verbs, and after other parts of speech, the infinitive is preceded by **zu**.

e.g. Ich versuche **zu studieren**.
I am trying to study.
Es ist schwer das Richtige **zu finden**.
It is difficult to find the right thing.

A particularly useful construction is **um ... zu** *in order to:*

Susan fährt nach Deutschland **um** ihr Deutsch **zu verbessern**.
Susan goes to Germany (in order) to improve her German.

The infinitive with **zu** can also be used to indicate that something can or cannot be done:

Der Chef ist im Moment nicht **zu finden**.
The boss is nowhere to be found at present.

In separable verbs, the **zu** is inserted between the compounds.

Ich habe Lust heute Abend aus**zu**gehen.
I feel like going out this evening.

○ The infinitive can also be used as a neuter noun; in this case, it is of course written with a capital letter.

(Das) Lernen macht mir Spaß.
I enjoy learning.

A》 Link the following sentences by using '*um ... zu ...*'.

e.g. Dieter geht nach Frankfurt. Er will dort studieren.
Dieter geht nach Frankfurt um dort zu studieren.

1 Roswitha schreibt an viele Firmen. Sie bewirbt sich um eine Stelle.
2 Hans besucht Leipzig. Er will die Lage dort sehen.
3 Die Freunde treffen sich in Roswithas Zimmer. Sie sprechen miteinander.
4 Ich fliege nach Berlin. Ich komme schneller an.
5 Ich kaufe eine Zeitung. Ich will sie im Flugzeug lesen.
6 Sie wählen zuerst 00 49 69. So können Sie Frankfurt von England aus direkt wählen.
7 Roswitha lernt viel. Sie will ein gutes Examen machen.
8 Hans macht Überstunden. Er will Geld für seinen Urlaub sparen.
9 Die Freunde fahren nach Bad Dürkheim. Sie wollen Susan den Wurstmarkt zeigen.
10 Hans trifft Carla auf der Hauptwache. Er will mit ihr ins Kino gehen.

B》 Use an infinitive construction to simplify the following.

e.g. Heute können Sie Herrn Schäfer nicht sprechen.
Herr Schäfer ist heute nicht zu sprechen.

1 Die Nummer kann ich im Telefonbuch nicht finden.
2 Sie können Herrn Beck unter einer anderen Nummer erreichen.
3 Das kann ich heute nicht machen.
4 Das kann ich nicht glauben.

C》 Instead of 'Willst du?', begin the following questions with 'Hast du Lust ..?'

e.g. Willst du ein Glas Bier trinken?
Hast du Lust ein Glas Bier zu trinken?

1 Willst du eine Radtour machen?
2 Willst du auf den Wurstmarkt nach Bad Dürkheim fahren?
3 Willst du heute abend ins Kino gehen?
4 Willst du die Geburtstagsgeschenke aufmachen?

8.3 The future

> Ich werde auch etwas Praktisches machen.
> Wenn du zu Hause bleibst, kommen wir dich besuchen.

○ German uses the present tense to talk about the future whenever it is clear to both speaker and listener that the future is meant. In the dialogue example:

> Wenn du zu Hause bleibst, kommen wir dich besuchen.
> *If you stay at home, we shall come and visit you.*

the whole conversation is about the future, so there is no need to indicate it again in the tense of the verb.

Some more examples:

> Ich schreibe den Brief heute Abend .
> *I will write the letter this evening.*
> Wir fahren nächstes Jahr nach Spanien.
> *We will go to Spain next year.*

○ Where the meaning would not otherwise be clear, and in more formal language, German talks about the future by using **werden** plus the infinitive at the end of the clause. The forms of **werden** are:

> ich werde
> du wirst
> er/sie/es wird
> wir/Sie/sie werden
> ihr werdet

e.g. Ich **werde** etwas Praktisches **machen.**
> *I shall do something practical.*

(because **Ich mache etwas Praktisches** could mean that (s)he is already doing it!)

> Wir werden sehen.
> *We shall see.*

○ Note that **werden** on its own means *to become.* It is very useful when talking about career hopes!

> Was möchtest du werden?
> *What would you like to be?*

○ German also uses **werden** plus the infinitive to express likelihood (irrespective of time); the adverb **wohl** is often added:

e.g. Das wird wohl sein Bruder sein.
That's probably his brother.
Sie wird wohl schon zu Hause sein.
She's probably at home by now.

≫ You now know the uses of 'ich will', 'ich möchte', and 'ich werde'. Decide which of them fits the following examples:

1 Roswitha studiert in Frankfurt. Sie (*would like to*) als Beraterin für Umweltprobleme arbeiten.
2 Sie (*wants to*) sich um eine Stelle in Rheinland-Pfalz bewerben.
3 Sie (*will*) im September anfangen.
4 Dieters Bruder arbeitet als Techniker bei der Post und (*wants to*) sein Fachabitur im Herbst machen.
5 Er (*would like to*) auf die Technische Hochschule in Aachen gehen.
6 Er (*will*) im Sommer viel für seine Prüfungen lernen.

Wenn du zu Hause bleibst, kommen wir dich besuchen

8.4 Conditions and wishes (subjunctive 2)

Ich würde schon immer etwas Neues finden.
Das wäre für unsere Zukunft auch notwendig.
meine Eltern hätten gern
wenn ich nur wüsste
Das wäre gut.
Ich wünschte, ich wäre schon fertig.

○ A straightforward condition is expressed in German using the present tense after **wenn:**

> Wenn du zu Hause bleibst, kommen wir dich besuchen.
> *If you stay at home, we shall come and visit you.*

○ But if the speaker is suggesting that something *might* happen, then in most cases the verb form is **ich würde, du würdest** etc. plus the infinitive at the end:

> Ich **würde** etwas Neues **finden.**
> *I would find something new (if I went on studying mathematics).*

The forms of **ich würde** are:

> ich würde
> du würdest
> er/sie/es würde
> wir/Sie/sie würden
> ihr würdet

○ **Würde** is an example of a *subjunctive* form. Geman has two subjunctive tenses, which are used to describe actions which might take place, and to repeat what someone else has said (see sections 12.2 and 12.3). They are sometimes referred to as present subjunctive and past subjunctive, because they are formed from the present and simple past; but these names are misleading because in modern German, the use of the two tenses has nothing to do with present or past time. **Würde** is an example of subjunctive 2.

○ With a small number of short verbs, German uses the subjunctive 2 form of the verb itself in conditional sentences. Subjunctive 2 is formed from the simple past, and takes the endings **-e, -est, -e, -en -et**. Where the stem vowel is **a, o** or **u**, an umlaut is added. With **haben**, the simple past is **ich hatte**, so subjunctive 2 is:

ich **hätte**	wir/Sie/sie **hätten**
du **hättest**	ihr **hättet**
er/sie/es **hätte**	

○ The other verbs with which subjunctive 2 is commonly used are:

sein	**ich wäre**	*I would be*
dürfen	**ich dürfte**	*I would be allowed to*
können	**ich könnte**	*I would be able to*
mögen	**ich möchte**	*I should like*
müssen	**ich müsste**	*I would have to*
sollen	**ich sollte**	*I should*
wollen	**ich wollte**	*I would want to*
bringen	**ich brächte**	*I would bring*
brauchen	**ich bräuchte**	*I would need*
gehen	**ich ginge**	*I would go*
kommen	**ich käme**	*I would come*
lassen	**ich ließe**	*I would let*
stehen	**ich stände**	*I would stand*
wissen	**ich wüsste**	*I would know*

e.g. Das wäre gut!	*That would be good.*
Wenn ich nur wüsste.	*If only I knew.*
Das wäre notwendig.	*That would be necessary.*
Meine Eltern hätten es gern.	*My parents would like that.*

○ The subjunctive 2 forms **hätte, könnte** and **wäre** are also sometimes used as a form of politeness.

e.g. Könntest du die Tür öffnen?	*Could you open the door?*
Ich hätte gern ...	*I should like ...*
Das wäre alles ...	*That would be (= is) all.*

○ With **wünschen**, German frequently uses a subjunctive 2 form **ich wünschte** (*I wish, I would wish*) to express the wish itself:

Ich wünschte, ich wäre schon fertig.
I wish I had finished (studying).

129

A》 What would you do if you won a large sum of money? A nice holiday perhaps? Rewrite the following, saying what you would do.

e.g. Du fährst nach Griechenland.
      Ich würde nach Griechenland fahren.

1 Du wohnst in einem schönen Hotel.
2 Du liegst in der Sonne.
3 Du isst Moussaka und trinkst Wein.
4 Du besuchst eine Insel.
5 Du triffst alte Freunde.

B》 More dreams! This time, start each sentence with 'ich wünschte, ...'

e.g. viel Geld haben
      Ich wünschte, ich hätte viel Geld.

Look back to the list on page 129 to see whether you can use a subjunctive 2; if not, you will need 'würde' plus the infinitive.

1 auf Urlaub sein
2 ein schönes Haus haben
3 in der Sonne liegen
4 viel essen und trinken können
5 mitfahren können
6 am Strand stehen
7 nie nach Hause fahren müssen

In der Sonne liegen

8.5 Word order for hypothesis

> könnte man die Abfälle umweltfreundlich beseitigen

○ In written German, it is not always necessary to start a condition or a hypothetical statement with **wenn** ... You can express the same meaning by starting with the verb itself in subjunctive 2.

e.g. Hätte er fleißiger studiert, so wäre er heute Ingenieur

means the same as:

> Wenn er fleißiger studiert hätte, ...
> *If he had studied more diligently ...*

English can sometimes use a similar construction (ie *had he studied more diligently, ...*) but this is a very literary style and seldom used. In German, this word order is far more common, especially in written reports.

Two more examples; in each case the English has to start with *if,* which is expressed in German by the word order:

> Hätte ich das gewusst, wäre ich nicht hingegangen.
> *If I had known that, I would not have gone.*

> Könnte man die Abfälle umweltfreundlicher beseitigen, so wäre dies ein großer Fortschritt.
> *If one could get rid of the waste in a more environmentally friendly manner, this would be a great step forward.*

The second clause in such sentences is frequently introduced by **so** or **dann**, but this is optional.

You will probably not wish to use this sort of construction in your own written German at this stage, but you should be prepared to recognise it and understand it when reading German.

》 How would you express the following in English?

1 Wäre sie krank, müsste ich allein kommen.
2 Hätte ich in der Schule mehr gelernt, könnte ich jetzt studieren.
3 Wäre ich so fleißig wie mein Bruder, dann könnte ich Ingenieur sein.
4 Hätte ich von der Party gewusst, dann wäre ich mitgekommen.
5 Käme er morgen nicht, so müssten wir ohne ihn feiern.
6 Wärst du bloß hier, so könnten wir zusammen feiern.

9 Being at the receiving end

17 Millionen Telegramme wurden aufgegeben

Die Deutsche Post

Roswitha, Susan und Dieter unterhalten sich über Briefe und
Telegramme.

Susan	Dieter, kannst du mir bitte helfen? Ich will diese Karte an eine Freundin in Frankreich schicken. Wie ist das mit der Postleitzahl?	
Dieter	Ganz einfach. **Man schreibt ein F** vor die französische Postleitzahl.	9.6
Susan	Und das gleiche bei anderen Ländern?	
Dieter	Natürlich. Für Österreich ein A, für die Schweiz CH und für England GB. **Dann wird alles automatisch sortiert**. Das **wurde vor einigen Jahren eingeführt**, ist inzwischen sehr **verbessert worden** und **lässt sich** noch weiter **verbessern**.	9.2 9.3 9.3 9.5
Roswitha	Du redest wie eine Werbung für die Deutsche Post! **Du interessierst dich** offensichtlich sehr für die Post — oder hat dir dein Bruder davon erzählt?	9.1

132

Dieter	Ja, weil er nämlich bei der Deutschen Post arbeitet. Wisst ihr, dass **der Briefverkehr** in Europa durch die deutsche und die französiche Post **dominiert wird?**

9.2

Susan	Was bedeutet das?
Dieter	**Fast die Hälfte des Briefverkehrs** in Europa **wird** von der deutschen und der französischen Post **befördert.** Dann gibt es noch die Telegramme.

9.2

Susan	Telegramme? **Inlandstelegramme wurden** in England schon vor Jahren **abgeschafft.**

9.3

Dieter	In Deutschland nicht. **Hier gibt es sie noch.**

9.4

Susan	Aber ich denke, alles **wird jetzt elektronisch, gemacht,** ich meine mit E-Mail und so weiter. Oder telefonisch.

9.2

Dieter	Nicht immer. Viele Leute lieben es immer noch, wenn ein Telegramm vom Postboten geliefert wird.
Roswitha	Aber früher war das doch viel wichtiger.
Dieter	Das schon. In der alten DDR besonders hatten nur wenige Menschen Telefon zu Hause. **Es wurde viel darüber geschimpft,** aber **es ließ sich nichts machen.** Da **wurde** halt ein Telegramm **geschickt.** Selbst kurz nach der Wiedervereinigung **wurden** in einem Jahr immer noch 17 Millionen Telegramme **aufgegeben.**

9.4
9.5
9.3
9.3

Susan	**Ich bin stark beeindruckt.** Und heute?

9.2

Dieter	Heutzutage hat fast jeder nicht nur Telefon zu Hause, sondern auch ein Handy. Telegramme **werden** vor allem nur zu besonderen Anlässen **geschickt.** Wer weiß aber, wie lange noch.

9.2

9.1 Reflexive verbs

du interessierst dich

○ A **reflexive verb** is one in which the subject is doing something to or for him/herself. Examples in English are:

> *I wash myself.*
> *I buy myself a coat.*

German also has reflexive verbs. The accusative is used if the action is done *to* the subject (i.e. if the subject is also the object), and the dative if it is something done *for* the subject (i.e. if something else is the object).

> Ich wasche **mich.**
> Ich kaufe **mir** einen Mantel.

German sometimes uses a reflexive where English does not:

> Ich interessiere **mich** für Sport.
> *I am interested in sport.*
> Ich erinnere **mich.**
> *I remember.*
> Ich irre **mich**
> *I make a mistake*

○ Most of the **reflexive pronouns** are the same as the personal pronouns (Unit 1). The only difference is that **sich** is used for the 3rd person (singular **er/sie/es** and plural **sie**) and the formal **Sie**.

Nom.	Acc. Personal	Acc. Reflexive	Dat. Personal	Dat. Reflexive
ich	mich	mich	mir	mir
du	dich	dich	dir	dir
er	ihn	**sich**	ihm	**sich**
sie (*she*)	sie	**sich**	ihr	**sich**
es	es	**sich**	ihm	**sich**
wir	uns	uns	uns	uns
sie (*they*)	sie	**sich**	ihnen	**sich**
Sie	Sie	**sich**	Ihnen	**sich**
ihr	euch	euch	euch	euch

e.g. ich erinnere mich   *I remember*
du erinnerst dich   *you remember*
er erinnert sich   *he remembers*
Sie erinnern sich   *you remember*

○ In the plural, the reflexive pronouns can also indicate *reciprocal* action, corresponding to the English *each other.*

Wir kennen uns.   *We know each other.*
Sie treffen sich.   *They meet (each other).*

A》 Insert the correct reflexive pronouns in the following sentences:

1 Susan interessiert ____ sehr für das deutsche Leben und die deutsche Kultur.
2 Ich setzte ____ auf den Stuhl.
3 Der Arbeiter freut ____ auf den Feierabend.
4 Die Firma nennt ____ arbeiterfreundlich.
5 Wie lange kennt ihr ____?
6 Wir kennen ____ schon lange.
7 Die Großmutter in Alzey erinnert ____ an die Tage kurz nach dem Krieg.
8 Ich kaufe ____ eine neue Jacke.
9 Hast du ____ schon die Zähne geputzt?

B》 The following description of Herr Schulz's move to Frankfurt contains several reflexive verbs:

sich sehnen   *to long for*
sich wohlfühlen   *to feel well*
sich einstellen auf   *to adjust to*
sich freuen auf   *to look forward to*
sich (etwas) vorstellen   *to imagine*

Insert the correct pronoun in each case:

Nach der Wende ist Herr Schulz nach Frankfurt umgezogen. Er fühlte ____ **(1)** sehr wohl, aber trotzdem sehnte er ____ **(2)** manchmal nach der alten Heimat. Seinen Freunden erklärte er das so: „Wir hatten ____ **(3)** schon auf mehr Freiheit eingestellt, wir hatten ____ **(4)** sehr auf das wiedervereinigte Deutschland gefreut, aber wir hatten ____ **(5)** die Wende nicht so krass vorgestellt."

9.2 The passive – present tense

> Dann wird alles automatisch sortiert.
> Fast die Hälfte des Briefverkehrs wird befördert.
> Der Briefverkehr wird dominiert.
> Alles wird jetzt elektronisch gemacht.
> Telegramme werden geschickt.
> Ich bin stark beeindruckt.

○ When you are talking about an action, and are more interested in what is being done than in who is doing it, you will tend to use what is known as *the passive*. In English this is formed from the verb *to be* and the past participle:

> *Everything is sorted automatically.*
> *Telegrams are sent.*

German forms the same construction but with the verb **werden.** The past participle goes to the end of the clause:

> Alles **wird** automatisch **sortiert.**
> Telegramme **werden geschickt.**

Some further examples:

> Ich **werde** für diese Arbeit **bezahlt.**
> *I am getting paid for this work.*
> Wir **werden** nicht **gefragt.**
> *We are not being asked.*

○ You can only form the passive from a verb which normally takes an accusative object. This object becomes the subject of the new sentence:

> Ich sortiere die Briefe.   *I sort the letters.*
> Die Briefe werden sortiert.   *The letters* are *sorted.*

English can make a passive from an indirect object:

> *She gives him a shirt.*
> *He is given a shirt.*

German cannot do this; the indirect object has to remain in the dative:

> Sie gibt **ihm** ein Hemd.
> **Ihm** wird ein Hemd gegeben.

The latter is so clumsy that you wouldn't use it!

○ Only if you are describing a state rather than an action can you use **sein** plus the past participle:

> Ich bin beeindruckt. *I am impressed.*

Compare:

> Die Bank ist geschlossen. *The bank is closed.*
> Die Bank wird geschlossen. *The bank is being closed (down).*

This creates difficulties for English-speaking learners who tend to use **sein** where it should be **werden.** In fact, in most cases, the verb you want will be **werden**!

A》 The following sentences describe different actions. Turn them round to passive forms, omitting the original subject.

e.g. Ich bestelle die Karten.
Die Karten werden bestellt.

1 Die Deutschen trinken viel Bier.
2 Mein Vater liest die Zeitung.
3 Ich nähe den Rock.
4 Wir mieten ein Auto.
5 Die Sekretärin reserviert das Hotelzimmer.
6 Sie schickt auch ein Telegramm.

B》 The following is an account of a letter's journey from writer to reader. Rewrite each sentence stressing the action rather than the doer, i.e. again using the passive.

e.g. Ich schreibe den Brief.
Der Brief wird geschrieben.

1 Ich schreibe die Adresse auf den Umschlag.
2 Auf die Rückseite schreibe ich den Absender.
3 Ich stecke den Brief in den Umschlag.
4 Mein Bruder trägt ihn zum Briefkasten.
5 Er steckt ihn in den Briefkasten.
6 Der Postbote holt alle Briefe vom Briefkasten ab.
7 Er fährt sie zur Post.
8 Dort sortiert man die Briefe automatisch.
9 Die Post schickt die Briefe an den Zustellungsort.
10 Der Briefträger stellt sie zu.
11 Mein Freund holt meinen Brief aus dem Briefkasten.
12 Er liest den Brief und schreibt eine Antwort.

9.3 The passive – past tenses

> Das wurde vor einigen Jahren eingeführt.
> 17 Millionen Telegramme wurden aufgegeben.
> Inlandstelegramme wurden abgeschafft.
> Da wurde ein Telegramm geschickt.
> Das ist inzwischen verbessert worden.

○ The simple past form of **werden** is **wurde**. So the simple past form of the passive is:

> ich **wurde** bezahlt
> es **wurde** geschickt etc.

This form is very common in accounts of past events.

> e.g. Es wurde vor einigen Jahren eingeführt.
> *It was introduced some years ago.*
>
> 17 Millionen Telegramme wurden geschickt.
> *17 million telegrams were sent.*
>
> Das Rathaus wurde 1887 gebaut.
> *The Town Hall was built in 1887.*

○ Be careful not to confuse **wurde** and **würde**. The form with umlaut means *would* and is dealt with in section 8.4.

○ The perfect passive form is composed of **sein ... worden.**

> e.g. Es ist geplant worden.
> *It has been planned.*

The perfect passive is seldom used! But you may meet it occasionally. Note that the participle is **worden** rather than **geworden**; the latter is only used when the verb **werden** is used in its own right as in:

> Es ist kühler geworden.
> *It has become cooler.*

○ Sometimes a passive is used even when the speaker wishes to indicate the doer of the action. English uses *by*; German uses **von** for the person doing the action, and **durch** for the means by which it is done.

> Das Haus wurde von meinem Großvater gekauft.
> *The house was bought by my grandfather.*

> Das Haus wurde durch ein Unwetter zerstört.
> *The house was damaged by a storm.*

Any object with which the action is done is introduced by **mit** as in English:

> Das Glas wurde mit Bier gefüllt.
> *The glass was filled with beer.*

A⟩⟩ Relate the following events from post-war German history in the past tense.

e.g. 7. Oktober 1949 Gründung der DDR
Am 7. Oktober 1949 wurde die DDR gegründet.

1	26. Mai 1952	Abriegelung der Grenze BRD-DDR
2	24. Juli 1952	Auflösung der fünf Länder in der DDR
3	13. August 1961	Bau der Berliner Mauer
4	2. Mai 1989	Beginn des Abbaus der Grenze Ungarn-Österreich
5	9. November 1989	Öffnung der Grenzen in Deutschland
6	1. Juli 1990	Einführung der D-Mark in der DDR
7	3. Oktober 1990	Wiedervereinigung Deutschlands

B⟩⟩ The following is a list of things which politicians promised to do after reunification. Say that each of them was, in fact, done gradually.

e.g. Wir werden die Straßen reparieren.
Die Straßen wurden allmählich repariert.

1 Wir werden neue Telefonanschlüsse schaffen.
2 Wir werden die Arbeitslosen wieder einstellen.
3 Wir werden die Häuser reparieren.
4 Wir werden die Lehrer umschulen.
5 Wir werden die Renten erhöhen.
6 Wir werden die Arbeitszeit angleichen.

C)» The old grandmother in Alzey tells Susan more about German wines. Insert into her narrative the correct form of 'werden' (present or past) and the verbs from the following list, which are given in the correct sequence:

1 anbauen; **2** bearbeiten; **3** zerstören; **4** anbauen; **5** abfüllen; **6** exportieren; **7** trinken; **8** auszeichnen; **9** verkaufen; **10** produzieren

In Deutschland _____ Wein nur in bestimmten Gegenden _____ (**1**). Früher _____ Weinberge auch entlang der Lahn und weiter nördlich _____ (**2**). Viele dieser Weinberge _____ im Dreißigjährigen Krieg _____ (**3**). Es gibt in vielen Orten noch Felder, die „Im Weingarten" heißen. Dort _____ früher Wein _____ (**4**). Hier in Rheinland-Pfalz _____ sehr viel Wein _____ (**5**). Er _____ auch _____ (**6**). In Deutschland _____ mehr Bier als Wein _____ (**7**), aber bei uns ist das anders. In unserem Haus trinkt man Wein. Einer unserer Weine _____ bei der letzten Weinprobe _____ (**8**). Er _____ nun als Kabinettwein _____ (**9**). Eiswein _____ bei uns nicht _____ (**10**).

D)» 'Von', 'durch' or 'mit'? Complete the gaps in the following sentences, and put the article into the correct case as appropriate.

1 Das Kleid wurde _____ (mein) Mutter genäht.
2 Das Kleid wurde _____ (die) Maschine genäht.
3 Während des Essens wurde Susans Kleid _____ Soße begossen.
4 Kurz nach der Wende wurde der damalige Bundeskanzler Kohl in den neuen Bundesländern _____ Tomaten beworfen.
5 Die Telefonleitungen wurden _____ (die) Telekom gelegt.
6 Der Weinberg wurde _____ (ein) Unwetter zerstört.

Meine Mutter näht das Kleid

9.4 Uses of the impersonal *es*

> Hier gibt es sie noch.   Es wurde viel darüber geschimpft.

○ The passive can be used to express an action in general, with no indication of who in particular is involved. The subject is an impersonal **es**.

e.g. Es wird viel gesungen und getanzt.
There is a lot of singing and dancing.

Es wurde viel darüber geschimpft.
There were a lot of complaints about it.

If the sentence starts with something other than the impersonal **es**, this is omitted altogether:

Auf den Straßen wird viel gesungen and getanzt.
In der alten DDR wurde viel darüber geschimpft.

○ There are other uses of the impersonal **es**. In particular, it is used with a small number of verbs where the subject is unspecific:

Es regnet.	*It is raining.*
Es schneit.	*It is snowing.*
Es zieht.	*There's a draught.*
Es tut mir leid.	*I am sorry.*
Es freut mich.	*I am pleased.*
Es geht mir gut.	*I am well.*

The impersonal **es** is used with **sein** und **werden.** In the singular, this corresponds to English usage so creates no problems:

Es ist der Briefträger.	*It's the postman.*
Es wird spät.	*It's getting late.*

But it can also be used in German with a plural verb:

Es sind Freunde von mir.	*They are friends of mine.*
Es waren eine halbe Million.	*There were half a million.*

The form **es gibt** with past **es gab** is another way of expressing the English *there is/are* and *there was/were*:

Es gibt Fax, E-Mail und Handys.
There is fax, e-mail and mobile phones.

Die gibt es bei uns nicht mehr.
We don't have them any more.

141

Note particularly:

a) **Es gibt** is followed by the accusative.

b) Where a specific place is mentioned, German uses **es ist/es sind** rather than **es gibt/es gab**.
    Es waren viele Leute im Postamt.
    There were a lot of people in the Post Office.

A⟩⟩ The following expressions all include or imply 'es'. How would you express them in English?

1   Es wurde bis Mitternacht getanzt.
2   In England wird es nicht so gemacht.
3   Jetzt wird geschlafen.
4   Morgen gibt es Eintopf.
5   Es waren viele Menschen auf der Straße.

B⟩⟩ Make the following daily working routine less personal by using passives or impersonal constructions. Some of the events can be converted into straightforward passives, because there is an object which can become the new subject.

e.g. Ich trinke Kaffee.
      Kaffee wird getrunken.

But others do not have a subject, so you will need an impersonal construction.

e.g. Ich stehe um 7 Uhr auf.
      Um 7 Uhr wird aufgestanden.

1   Um 8.30 Uhr dusche ich.
2   Ich esse mein Frühstück.
3   Ich fahre zur Arbeit.
4   Ich lese die Post.
5   Ich diktiere die Briefe.
6   Um 12 Uhr mache ich Mittagspause.
7   Ich gehe in ein Restaurant.
8   Ich esse gut.
9   Ich schreibe einen Bericht.
10 Ich gehe nach Hause.

9.5 Uses of *lassen*

> Es lässt sich noch weiter verbessern.
> Es ließ sich nichts machen.

○ **Lassen** has three main areas of meaning. Firstly, it can mean to leave or to leave behind:

> Ich habe mein Auto auf dem Parkplatz gelassen.
> *I have left my car in the car park.*

In this context, it can form some frequently-used combinations, e.g. **liegen lassen, stehen lassen** and **fallen lassen.** In these, and when used with other verbs (see below), the past participle is formed without the prefix **ge-**:

> Ich habe meine Schlüssel liegen lassen.
> *I have left my keys lying about.*

> Ich habe den Kaffee stehen lassen.
> *I left the coffee standing.*

> Ich habe die Vase fallen lassen.
> *I dropped the vase.*

○ **Lassen** is also used with other verbs to mean *let* or *allow*:

> Lass mich mal sehen.   *Let me have a look.*
> Er lässt seinen Hund immer bellen!   *He always lets his dog bark.*

Frequently, it is used with a reflexive pronoun to imply that something can be done:

> Das lässt sich schnell machen.   *That can soon be done.*
> Es lässt sich noch weiter verbessern.   *It can be further improved.*
> Es ließ sich nichts machen.   *Nothing could be done.*

Note that although English uses a passive here, German keeps to the infinitive for the second verb.

○ Finally, **lassen** can be used to mean *to make someone else do something,* or *to have something done.* Here again, the second verb is in the infinitive whereas English uses a past participle:

> Ich lasse das Auto reparieren.   *I am having the car repaired.*
> Ich lasse mir die Haare schneiden.   *I am having my hair cut.*

143

A⟩⟩ The following statements indicate who can do various jobs. Use 'lassen' to say that you will have them done.

e.g. Der Schuster kann die Schuhe reparieren.
      Ich lasse den Schuster die Schuhe reparieren.

1   Der Automechaniker kann mein Auto reparieren.
2   Der Elektriker kann unseren Toaster reparieren.
3   Meine Schwester kann meinen Computer reparieren.
4   Die Sekretärin kann den Brief schreiben.
5   Der Maler kann das Zimmer tapezieren.
6   Meine Mutter kann das Kleid nähen.
7   Der Friseur kann die Haare schneiden.
8   Mein Sohn kann das Essen machen.
9   Die Spülmaschine kann das Geschirr abwaschen.
10 Der Gärtner kann den Rasen mähen.
11 Der Klempner kann die Wasserleitung reparieren.

B⟩⟩ How would you express the following in English?

1   Er hat mich warten lassen.
2   Das lässt sich nicht leugnen.
3   Lass mich in Ruhe!
4   Der Chef hat den Abteilungsleiter kommen lassen.
5   Das lasse ich mir nicht gefallen.
6   Ich lasse es mir sofort bringen.

Der Gärtner kann den Rasen mähen

9.6 Alternatives to the passive

Man schreibt ein F vor die Postleitzahl.

- German has a number of alternative constructions which are frequently used where English prefers a passive. The most important of these involves the word **man**, which translates literally as *one* but has none of the upper-class overtones of the English word. It is impersonal and should not be confused with **der Mann** (*the man*):

  > Man schreibt ein F vor die Postleitzahl.
  > *An F is written in front of the postcode.*
  > (OR *You write an F in front of the postcode.*)

- Because the German object may precede the verb, this too can be used where English would naturally adopt a passive:

  > Diesen Titel gibt der Verlag Bertelsmann heraus.
  > *This title is published by Bertelsmann Verlag.*

- The verb **sein** followed by **zu** and the infinitive also has a passive meaning:

  > Dieser Text ist bis morgen zu übersetzen.
  > *This text is to be translated by tomorrow.*

  > Es war niemand zu sehen.
  > *Nobody was to be seen.*

>> Express the following more simply using 'man':

1 Die Post wird automatisch sortiert.
2 Hier darf nicht geraucht werden.
3 Die Firma wurde verstaatlicht.
4 Das System ist verbessert worden.
5 Inlandstelegramme wurden abgeschafft.

10 Descriptions

Kurze Röcke trage ich gem

Im Jugendmodehaus

Susan, Carla und Roswitha gehen ins Jugendmodehaus **auf der Frankfurter Zeil** einkaufen.   10.2

Carla	**Diese weiße Bluse steht dir** aber wirklich **gut.** Sie passt dir **am besten** von all den vielen Sachen, die du anprobiert hast. Schade, **dass** ich nicht so **schlank** bin wie du, sonst würde ich sie auch mal anprobieren.	10.2 / 10.6 10.8 10.1
Susan	**Der braune Rock** passt dir tatsächlich wie angegossen. Der macht eine gute Figur. Und so **ein schöner Schnitt.** Vielleicht **etwas zu lang.** In England habe ich **etwas Ähnliches,** aber **meiner** ist **etwas kürzer.**	10.2 10.3 / 10.1 10.9 10.4 / 10.8
Carla	Stimmt. **Kurze Röcke** trage ich auch gern. Aber das ist **kein großes Problem**, ich kann ihn selbst kürzen. Aber sieh mal auf **das dumme Preisschild!** Das wäre **das teuerste Kleidungsstück**, das ich mir je gekauft habe.	10.3 10.3 10.2 / 10.8

146

Roswitha	Der Rock ist **ehrlich klasse**. Der steht dir richtig gut. Den würde ich nehmen.	10.6
Carla	Und bezahlen? Dann hätte ich ja **keinen einzigen Pfennig für** den Rest des Monats.	10.2
Roswitha	Carla, **die ewig Jammernde**. Frag **doch mal deine liebe Mutter**! Für **etwas Elegantes** legt **die Gute** bestimmt **ein kleines Sümmchen** dazu.	10.9 / 10.7 10.2 / 10.9 10.9 / 10.3
Carla	**Deine** vielleicht, aber **meine** bestimmt nicht! **Du kennst sie ja**. Und übrigens, **wir müssen** uns **schon** beeilen. Wir wollten **doch** Hans **treffen**. Er braucht **neue Schuhe**. Wir wollten ihn um drei im Schuhgeschäft treffen. Ich nehme **den braunen Rock** und laufe schon rasch vor.	10.4 10.7 10.7 10.3 10.2
Roswitha	Ich wollte auch noch **schnell** zum Jeans Palast gehen. Ich suche zu dieser Jacke **passende Jeans**. Vielleicht brauche ich auch nichts. Ich bin ja auch mal wieder **vollkommen pleite**.	10.6 10.5 10.6
Susan	Was hältst du **denn von der weißen Bluse** hier?	10.7 / 10.2
Roswitha	Oh, ich weiß nicht so ganz. **So schön** wie Carlas Rock **ist sie nicht**. Und **sündhaft teuer**, meinst du nicht?	10.1 10.6
Susan	Das glaube ich auch, dann nehme ich sie nicht. Carla wird mich wohl „die sparsame Susan" nennen, aber die Bluse ist **nicht besonders schön** und **sehr, sehr teuer**.	10.1 / 10.6 10.1 / 10.6
Roswitha	Soll ich dir schnell **ein aufmunterndes Eis** kaufen, so als Trost? Aber wir müssen uns schon beeilen. Carla und Hans **warten bestimmt** schon auf uns, und Hans ist **eben** nicht gerade **der Geduldigste**.	10.5 10.6 10.7 10.9

10.1 Free-standing adjectives

> dass ich nicht so schlank bin   etwas zu lang
> so schön ist sie nicht   nicht besonders schön
> sehr, sehr teuer

○ An *adjective* is a word which gives further information about a noun. Adjectives are used to indicate size, colour, temperature, mood etc. Examples of adjectives in English are *big, red, hot, angry*.

○ Adjectives may be either free-standing or linked to the noun. For example, in English we can say:

> The blouse is *white*.
> OR   The *white* blouse suits you.

In the first sentence, the adjective is *free-standing*; in the second it is linked to the noun, it forms part of a **noun phrase**.

○ In German, free-standing adjectives do not require any endings.

Some examples from our dialogue:

> Die Bluse ist nicht besonders **schön** und sehr **teuer.**
> *The blouse is not particularly nice, and very expensive.*

> So **schön** ist sie nicht.
> *It is not that nice.*

> Schade, dass ich nicht so **schlank** bin.
> *A pity that I am not so slim.*

A⟩⟩ Find the opposites of the following adjectives:

1   kalt
2   ruhig
3   groß
4   intelligent
5   traurig
6   neu
7   interessant
8   modern
9   schnell
10   teuer

B)〉 Find an appropriate adjective to fit the following sentences:

1 In Deutschland sind die Briefkästen _____.
2 Die Bluse gefällt mir, aber sie ist sehr _____.
3 Neue Schuhe sind oft _____.
4 Das Haus ist sehr _____; es stammt aus dem 15. Jahrhundert.
5 Ältere Menschen finden Popmusik zu _____.
6 Als Herr Schulz nach Frankfurt kam, war ihm das Leben in Westen sehr _____.

10.2 Adjectives used with secondary endings

diese weiße Bluse	der braune Rock
den braunen Rock	das dumme Preisschild
keinen einzigen Pfennig	deine liebe Mutter
auf der Frankfurter Zeil	von der weißen Bluse

○ Where an adjective in German is used as part of a noun phrase, it will take an ending. Provided that *some other element* in the phrase, i.e. either the determiner or the noun itself, *has an ending which indicates case and singular/plural*, the adjective will end in:

-e **in the nominative singular**
-en **elsewhere (i.e. masculine singular accusative and all datives, genitives and plurals)**

(For adjectives where no other element indicates case and number, and for a reference table, see section 10.3)

In the following examples, the case/number marker is underlined and the adjective ending is in bold.

de<u>r</u> braun**e** Rock	*the brown skirt*
da<u>s</u> dumm**e** Preisschild	*the silly price ticket*
dies<u>e</u> weiß**e** Bluse	*this white blouse*
ich kaufe de<u>n</u> braun**en** Rock	*I'll buy the brown skirt* (acc.)
dein<u>e</u> lieb**e** Mutter	*your dear mother*
ich habe kein<u>en</u> einzig**en** Pfennig	*I haven't a single Pfennig* (acc.)
von de<u>r</u> weiß**en** Bluse	*of the white blouse* (dat.)

149

Some further examples:

mit de<u>m</u> nächst**en** Zug	*with the next train* (dat.)
di<u>e</u> best**en** Studenten	*the best students* (pl.)
mein<u>e</u> neu**en** Schuhe	*my new shoes* (pl.)
de<u>s</u> neu**en** Chefs	*of the new boss* (gen.)
eine Flasche gut**en** Wein<u>s</u>	*a bottle of good wine* (gen.)

○ A small number of adjectives do not take any ending:

a) Adjectives ending in **-er** derived from town names:

die Frankfurter Zeil	*the Zeil (street) in Frankfurt*
die Berliner Mauer	*the Berlin Wall*

The only country name which can take an **-er** ending is **die Schweiz**, from which you have an adjective **Schweizer** written with a capital letter and without endings, e.g. **Schweizer Käse**. There is also a less common adjective **schweizerisch**, which does take endings.

b) Adjectives ending in **-er** derived from numerals:

die achtziger Jahre	*the eighties*

c) Names of colours imported from other languages and ending in a vowel

e.g. lila *lilac* orange *orange*

die lila Jacke	*the lilac jacket*

But there are alternatives in **-farben** or **-farbig** (*-coloured*) which do take endings and are frequently used:

das orangefarbene Kleid	*the orange-coloured dress*

》 In the following examples, decide whether the adjective will end in '-e', '-en' or '-er' or whether it will have no ending at all.

1 Der (kalt) Krieg dauerte von 1945 bis 1989.
2 Ich kaufe diesen (rot) Mantel.
3 Ich fahre gern mit der (London) U-Bahn.
4 Die (alt) Dame ist sehr (nett).
5 Sie ist die Schwester meiner (alt) Deutschlehrerin.
6 Die (groß) Gläser sind für Bier, nicht für Wein!
7 Das (neu) Rathaus wurde 1890 gebaut.
8 Im (alt) Rathaus ist jetzt ein Museum.
9 Meine (neu) Freundin kommt aus Manchester.
10 Ich gehe mit meiner (neu) Freundin ins Kino.

10.3 Adjectives with primary endings

ein schöner Schnitt	kein großes Problem
ein kleines Sümmchen	neue Schuhe
kurze Röcke	

○ Where the adjective forms part of a noun phrase and there is no other case or number marker, the adjective itself has to show both case and number. The endings are the same as those of **dieser.**

	Masculine	Neuter	Feminine	Plural
Nominative	dies**er**	dies**es**	dies**e**	dies**e**
Accusative	dies**en**			
Dative	dies**em**	dies**em**	dies**er**	dies**en**
Genitive	dies**es**	dies**es**	dies**er**	dies**er**

This situation occurs:

a) where there is no determiner, and

b) where the determiner has no ending (see sections 3.1 and 3.2). This applies in the nominative singular masculine and neuter of **ein, kein, mein, dein, sein, ihr, unser, euer** and **Ihr.** Note that in **unser** and **euer,** the **-er** is not an ending, it is part of the stem!

○ The following examples from our dialogue illustrate the point. The adjective endings are in bold type:

neu**e** Schuhe	*new shoes*
kurz**e** Röcke	*short skirts*
ein schön**er** Schnitt	*a nice cut*
kein groß**es** Problem	*not a big problem*
ein klein**es** Sümmchen	*a small sum*

The following sets of examples illustrate the basic rule:

If nothing else has a marker showing number and case, the adjective will. (primary endings)

If anything else has a marker showing number and case, the adjective ends in **-e** (nom. sing.) or **-en** (elsewhere) (secondary endings)

gut**er** Wein	*good wine*
ein gut**er** Wein	*a good wine*
d<u>er</u> gut**e** Wein	*the good wine*
mit gut**em** Wein	*with good wine*
mit ein<u>em</u> gut**en** Wein	*with a good wine*
mit d<u>em</u> gut**en** Wein	*with the good wine*

○ The following points may be noted:

a) In the masculine and neuter genitive singular, the noun itself takes an **-s** marker; consequently none is needed on the adjective even if there is no determiner.

> e.g. gut**en** Wein<u>s</u> (secondary ending because the <u>s</u> is already there on the noun)

Similarly in the dative plural, the noun itself takes the **-n** marker

> e.g. mit schön**en** Kleider<u>n</u> (secondary ending because the <u>-n</u> is already there on the noun).

b) The adjectives **viel** (*much*) and **wenig** (*little*) are mostly used without endings in the singular, but with primary endings in the plural.

> e.g. viel Musik   *a lot of music*
>
>   wenige Menschen   *few people*
>
>   viel Geld   *a lot of money*

Less frequently, they follow another determiner in which case they take secondary endings

> das viele Geld   *the large amount of money*

c) In the plural, **alle** and **sämtliche** (both meaning *all*) are regarded as ordinary determiners and are followed by secondary endings. But numbers are not determiners; they are followed by primary endings.

> e.g. alle billig**en** Kleider
>
>   vier billig**e** Kleider

d)   With adjectives which only partially 'determine' which nouns you are talking about, Germans are sometimes unsure which endings to use:

After **einige** (*some*), **viele** (*many*), **mehrere** (*several*) and **wenige** (*few*), primary endings are the rule, and this is usually the case after **manche** (*some*).

After **solche** (*such*) and **beide** (*both*), secondary endings are more frequent.

》 In the following statements overheard in the 'Jugendmodehaus', decide whether the adjective needs to show the marker or whether it is shown elsewhere. Then supply the appropriate ending.

1   Diesen (schick) Rock kann ich Ihnen sehr empfehlen.
2   Die (schwarz) Bluse passt sehr gut zu dem (rot) Rock.
3   Ich suche eine (schwarz) Jacke.
4   Ich suche ein (weiß) Hemd.
5   Das ist ein sehr (elegant) Stück.
6   Zu dieser (schön) Bluse kann ich Ihnen auch einen (modisch) Rock empfehlen.
7   (Elegant) Kleider sind schwer zu finden.
8   Kaufst du dieses (schön) Kleid? Ja, ich brauche ein (neu) Kleid.
9   Zu meiner (schön) Bluse trage ich einen (neu) Rock und eine (golden) Kette.
10   Zu der (schwarz) Hose trage ich einen (los) Pulli und einen (breit) Gürtel.

Reiche Leute haben viel Geld

Reference table: Adjective endings

	Marker elsewhere Secondary endings in -e or -er			No other marker Primary endings		

Nominative

Masculine	der	gut **e**	Stoff		gut **er**	Stoff
				ein	gut **er**	Stoff
Neuter	das	echt **e**	Leder		echt **es**	Leder
				ein	echt **es**	Leder
Feminine	die	rein **e**	Wolle		rein **e**	Wolle
	eine	rein **e**	Wolle			
Plural	die	schön **en**	Kleider		schön **e**	Kleider
	meine	schön **en**	Kleider			

Accusative

Masculine	den	gut **en**	Stoff		gut **en**	Stoff
	einen	gut **en**	Stoff			

Determiners with no ending in the nominative singular (masculine and neuter):

ein   mein   dein   sein   kein   ihr   Ihr   unser   euer

		Marker elsewhere Secondary endings in –e or -er			No other marker Primary endings		

Dative

Masculine	dem	gut	**en**	Stoff	gut	**em**	Stoff
	einem	gut	**en**	Stoff			
Neuter	dem	echt	**en**	Leder	echt	**em**	Leder
	einem	echt	**en**	Leder			
Feminine	der	rein	**en**	Wolle	rein	**er**	Wolle
	einer	rein	**en**	Wolle			
Plural	den	schön	**en**	Kleidern			
	meinen	schön	**en**	Kleidern			
		schön	**en**	Kleidern			

Genitive

Masculine	des	gut	**en**	Stoffs			
	eines	gut	**en**	Stoffs			
		gut	**en**	Stoffs			
Neuter	des	echt	**en**	Leders			
	eines	echt	**en**	Leders			
		echt	**en**	Leders			
Feminine	der	rein	**en**	Wolle	rein	**er**	Wolle
	einer	rein	**en**	Wolle			
Plural	der	schön	**en**	Kleider	schön	**er**	Kleider
	meiner	schön	**en**	Kleider			

Adjective endings:
Rules and examples to remember

Where an adjective immediately precedes a noun, and there is
- no determiner OR
- the determiner is **ein, kein, mein, dein, sein, ihr, unser** or **Ihr**
  the adjective will take a primary ending (the same endings as **dieser**):

gut**er** Stoff
ein gut**er** Stoff

echt**es** Leder
ein echt**es** Leder

schön**e** Kleider
aus echt**em** Leder

Where an adjective follows any determiner other than those listed above OR
where the noun following the adjective has a genitive **-s**
the adjective will take a secondary ending, i.e.

-e for the nominative singular
-en everywhere else.

der gut**e** Stoff
das echt**e** Leder

mit dem echt**en** Leder
echt**en** Leders

Free-standing adjectives (i.e. separate from their noun) take no ending:

Das Leder ist echt.

10.4 Determiners with primary endings

> meiner ist etwas kürzer   deine vielleicht, aber meine nicht

○ The determiners **ein, kein, mein, dein, sein** etc. normally have no markers in the nominative singular masculine and neuter. But they can also be used as pronouns, and then take primary endings.

Masc. sing.	neuter. sing	fem. sing plural	
einer	**eins**	**eine**	*one*
keiner	**keins**	**keine**	*no-one, none*
meiner	**meins**	**meine**	*mine*
deiner	**deins**	**deine**	*yours (fam.)*
seiner	**seins**	**seine**	*his*
ihrer	**ihres**	**ihre**	*hers, theirs*

In the feminine, the pronoun form is the same as that of the determiner (i.e. ending in **-e**). But in the masculine and neuter, the primary ending must be added.

Compare

mein Rock   Mein**er** ist kürzer
my skirt   *Mine is shorter*

ein Hemd   Hier ist ein**s**
a shirt   *Here is one*

In the accusative, dative and genitive, the pronoun form is again identical with the possessive determiner.

eg.   Kaufst du einen Rock? Ich kaufe auch einen.
Are you buying a skirt? I'm also buying one.

》 In the following sentences, some of the determiners are used as pronouns – but not all! Some are simply determiners. Decide on the correct ending (if any!) in each case.

e.g.   Dein__ Rock ist kurz, aber mein__ ist noch kürzer
Dein Rock ist kurz, aber meiner ist noch kürzer

1   Mein__ Rock ist lang, aber dein__ ist noch länger.
2   Mein__ Bluse ist schön, aber dein__ ist noch schöner!

3 Du kaufst ein__ Eis? Ich möchte auch ein__!
4 Hast du ein__ Auto? Nein, ich habe kein__
5 Dein__ Vater ist sparsam? Mein___ auch!
6 Hans und Maria haben ihre Autos getauscht! Er fährt jetzt ihr__ und sie fährt sein__!

10.5 Participles as adjectives

passende Jeans   ein aufmunterndes Eis

○ We have already encountered the **past participle** in Units 7 and 9. It can also be used as an adjective, in which case it will take the same endings as any other adjective:

der verlorene Koffer	*the lost suitcase*
ein verlorener Koffer	*a lost suitcase*

Some past participles have taken on a meaning of their own as adjectives which differ from the original verb. These include:

ausgezeichnet	*excellent*
bekannt	*famous*
verrückt	*mad*

○ The **present participle** corresponds to the English form ending in '-ing' and consists of the infinitive with an additional **-d**. So from **singen** the present participle is **singend**:

ein singender Polizist	*a singing policeman*

Examples from our dialogue:

passende Jeans	*matching jeans*
ein aufmunterndes Eis	*an ice-cream to cheer us up*

Among present participles with their own meaning are:

abwesend	*absent*
dringend	*urgent*
spannend	*exciting*
umfassend	*comprehensive*

○ Where the present participle has developed its own meaning, it can be used after the verb **sein.**

   e.g. Der Film war spannend.   *The film was exciting.*

   Ordinary present participles cannot be used in this way. Remember that (as pointed out in section 1.2) the only way of translating *he is singing* into German is **er singt.**

○ Especially in written German, it is possible to use the participles as the basis for a long phrase; the words dependent on the participle precede it. These phrases are often difficult to translate into English.

   e.g. ein mehrere Seiten umfassendes Buch
         a book comprising several pages

         das bis an den Rand gefüllte Glas
         the glass filled to the brim

》 Fit the past or present participles of the following verbs into the sentences so as to make sense:

strahlen spielen umfassen stehlen kochen führen

1   Im Goethehaus in Weimar ist die 5000 Bücher _____ Bibliothek des Dichters.
2   Ein _____ Kind sollte man in Ruhe lassen.
3   Zum Frühstück esse ich gerne ein _____ Ei.
4   Weimar spielte jahrhundertelang eine _____ Rolle in der deutschen Kultur.
5   Die Polizei sucht ein _____ Auto.
6   Roswitha kommt _____ mit ihrem neuen Rock aus dem Geschäft.

Ein aufmunterndes Eis

10.6 Adverbs

schnell gehen	sündhaft teuer	ehrlich klasse
vollkommen pleite	steht dir gut	besonders schön
sehr, sehr teuer	sie warten bestimmt	

○ **Adverbs** are used to expand the meaning of a verb, or of an adjective, or the sentence as a whole. They indicate place, time, manner etc.

In English, adverbs normally end in '-ly', e.g. *quickly, slowly, politely.* German uses no such suffix; virtually any adjective in German can also be used as an adverb.

e.g. Die Bluse steht dir **gut.**   *The blouse suits you well.*
Der Rock ist **ehrlich** klasse.   *The skirt is really great.*
Ich gehe **schnell** zum   *I am just popping into the*
Jeans Palast.   *Jeans Palast.*
sündhaft teuer   *sinfully expensive*
vollkommen pleite   *completely broke*
recht interessant   *really interesting*
wenig besser   *little better*

○ There are also adverbs in German which can only be used as such and not as adjectives. One such is **sehr** meaning *very.*

e.g. **sehr, sehr** teuer   *very, very expensive*
Another is **kaum**, meaning *hardly, scarcely.*

Others have slightly different forms, e.g. **besonders** (*specially*) where the adjective is **besondere**.

nicht **besonders** schön   *not particularly beautiful*

Frequently, a German adverb will express an idea for which English would use another construction. Among the most important are:

Sie warten **bestimmt**.   *They are sure to be waiting.*
Ich trinke **gern** Tee.   *I like drinking tea.*
Ich trinke **lieber** Kaffee.   *I prefer drinking coffee.*
Du kannst **ruhig** hierbleiben.   *You're welcome to stay.*
Sie aß **weiter**.   *She went on eating.*

○ Two suffixes which German does use to form adverbs are **-weise** and **-maßen.**

    e.g. beispielsweise   *for example*
            möglicherweise *possibly*
            einigermaßen   *to some extent*

» Find suitable adverbs for the following sentences:

  1   Carla spielt _____ Klavier.
  2   Deutsche Autofahrer fahren _____ viel zu _____.
  3   Viele Menschen essen _____ Schwarzwälder Kirschtorte.
  4   Wir haben noch Zeit. Lesen Sie _____ _____.
  5   Das Kleid sieht _____ gut aus.

Vollkommen pleite

10.7 Flavouring adverbs

Frag doch mal deine liebe Mutter.
Du kennst sie ja.
Wir wollen doch Hans treffen.
Wir müssen uns schon beeilen.
Was hältst du denn von der Bluse?
Hans ist eben nicht gerade der Geduldigste.

○ Some adverbs can be used without a specific meaning but alter the tone of a sentence or question as a whole. When used in this way, they are sometimes referred to as *flavouring particles* or *modal particles.* The resulting sentences are often very difficult to translate into English!

Some examples are:

doch   intensifies the urgency of an imperative:
Frag **doch** mal deine liebe Mutter.
Go on, ask your mother.

reminds the listener of something s/he should already know:
Wir wollen **doch** Hans treffen.
(Remember that) we want to meet up with Hans.

denn   makes questions sound less abrupt:
Was hältst du **denn** von der Bluse?
So what do you think of the blouse?

expresses surprise:
Kommst du **denn** nicht mit?
Aren't you coming? (I thought you were.)

eben   reinforces an inescapable conclusion:
Hans ist **eben** nicht gerade der Geduldigste.
Hans, alas, isn't the most patient of people.

in imperatives, suggests there is no real alternative:
Dann kauf **eben** die Bluse.
Then go ahead and buy the blouse (i.e. there is nothing else worth buying).

ja   appeals for agreement:
Du kennst sie **ja**!
Surely you know what she's like!

insists that what the speaker says is correct:
Wir haben **ja** darüber gesprochen.
But we spoke about that earlier.

in exclamations, adds a measure of surprise:
Heute ist es **ja** kalt!
Goodness, it is cold today!

mal   adds a sense of casualness:
Frag **mal** deine Mutter.
Try asking your mother.

schon adds an insistent note:
Wir müssen uns **schon** beeilen.
We'd better hurrry up.

expresses confidence:
Er wird **schon** bald da sein.
He'll soon be here (I'm sure).

○   Note that all these words also have many more uses, including as straightforward adverbs. Look them up in a good dictionary; you may be surprised how many possible uses there are.

》 Express the following thoughts using a flavouring adverb. You are talking to a close friend.

1   You know my brother of old!
2   Go on, have (drink) another cup of tea.
3   So where do you come from?
4   Golly, that dress is expensive!
5   I'm afraid clothes do cost money.
6   Come along!

10.8 Comparatives and superlatives

am besten	etwas kürzer	das teuerste Kleidungsstück

○ In English we can say that something is *bigger* or *the biggest*. These forms are known respectively as the **comparative** and **superlative** forms.

German also forms comparatives with **-er** and superlatives with **-st** or **-est**. Unlike English, German can do this with any adjective. English has adjectives such as *interesting*, where we cannot just add '-er', we have to say *more interesting* and *most interesting*. In German it is simply **interessanter** and **der/die/das interessanteste**.

Examples from the dialogue:

etwas **kürzer**	*a bit shorter*
das **teuerste** Kleidungsstück	*the most expensive item*

○ Where comparatives and superlatives are used as part of a noun phrase, they take the same endings as any other adjectives.

ein billiger**es** Hemd	*a cheaper shirt*
das billigst**e** Hemd	*the cheapest shirt*

However, they are frequently used as adverbs or in a free-standing position. With the comparative, this makes things easier because there are no endings to worry about.

Dieses Hemd ist billig**er**.   *This shirt is cheaper.*

But when superlatives are free-standing or used as adverbs, German uses the form **am ...-sten**.

Dieses Hemd ist **am** billig**sten**.   *This shirt is the cheapest.*

○ Short adjectives often add an umlaut in the comparative and superlative forms, e.g.

alt (*old*)	älter	am ältesten
jung (*young*)	jünger	am jüngsten
lang (*long*)	länger	am längsten
kurz (*short*)	kürzer	am kürzesten
warm (*hot, warm*)	wärmer	am wärmsten
kalt (*cold*)	kälter	am kältesten
groß (*big*)	größer	am größten

There are also some very important irregular forms:

gern (*gladly*)	lieber	am liebsten
gut (*gut*)	besser	am besten
hoch (*high*)	höher	am höchsten
nah (*near*)	näher	am nächsten
viel (*much*)	mehr	am meisten

○ In comparisons, the German equivalent for *than* is **als**:

Der Rhein ist länger als die Themse.
The Rhine is longer than the Thames.

○ To express ...*of all*, German puts **aller-** before the superlative:

am allerbesten	*best of all*
der allerhöchste Berg	*the highest mountain of all*

》 The following lists are all given in increasing values. Make sentences using the information in brackets.

e.g. (teuer)   Bier—Wein—Sekt
    Wein ist teurer als Bier, aber Sekt ist am teuersten.

1	(schnell)	Straßenbahn—Auto—Zug
2	(gut)	Popmusik—Jazz—klassische Musik
3	(fleißig)	ich—Praktikant—Chef
4	(hoch)	Westerwald—die Alpen—der Himalaya
5	(alt)	Hans—Elfriede—Oma
6	(jung)	Oma—Elfriede—Hans
7	(warm)	Winter— Frühjahr—Sommer
8	(kurz)	eine Stunde—eine Minute—eine Sekunde
9	(alt)	der Islam—das Christentum—der Judaismus
10	(lang schlafen)	Roswitha—Hans—Dieter
11	(gut schmecken)	Käse—Wurst—Kuchen
12	(umweltfreundlich)	mit dem Auto—mit dem Zug—zu Fuß gehen

10.9 Adjectives as nouns

die Gute	der Geduldigste	etwas Elegantes
Carla, die ewig Jammernde		etwas Ähnliches

○ Adjectives can also be used as nouns. For example, **die Gute** *the good lady,* **der Fremde** *the stranger.* They are written with a capital letter because they are nouns, but keep the adjective endings because they are adjectives!

der/die Fremd**e**	*the stranger* (m./f.)
ein Fremd**er**	*a stranger* (m.)
eine Fremd**e**	*a stranger* (f.)
die Fremd**en**	*the strangers* (pl.)

Similarly, nouns can be formed from participles:

der/die ewig Jammernd**e**	*the constant complainer* (m./f.)
ein Bekannt**er** von mir	*a friend of mine* (m.)
eine Bekannt**e** von mir	*a friend of mine* (f.)
meine Bekannt**en**	*my friends*

and from comparative or superlative forms:

der Geduldig**ste**	*the most patient* (*of people*)

○ After **etwas, nichts, viel** or **wenig,** adjectives are used as neuter singular nouns (written, of course, with a capital letter).

nichts Neues	*nothing new*
etwas Elegantes	*something elegant*

A》 Make nouns from the adjectives in brackets in the following sentences:

1 „Der (alt)" ist eine bekannte deutsche Fernsehsendung.
2 Die Firma hat 200 (angestellt).
3 Er ist (angestellt) bei Siemens.
4 Sie hat mir etwas (interessant) erzählt.
5 Mein (bekannt) wohnt in München.

B)> Susan would also like to buy some new clothes before returning to England. Can you complete the following account with the correct adjective forms? Careful: some are free-standing!

Susan möchte sich gerne eine (**1** neu) Bluse kaufen. Sie geht mit Carla und Roswitha in ein (**2** schön) Geschäft auf der Zeil. Es gibt eine (**3** groß) Auswahl von (**4** viel) (**5** schön) Kleidungsstücken. Sie probiert (**6** verschieden) Sachen an: einen (**7** gelb) Rock, einen (**8** breit) Gürtel, eine (**9** eng) Hose, eine (**10** schick) Bluse und ein (**11** elegant) Kleid. Sie nimmt nichts, denn der (**12** gelb) Rock ist ein bisschen zu (**13** empfindlich), der (**14** breit) Gürtel ist zu (**15** altmodisch), die (**16** eng) Hose steht ihr nicht, die (**17** schick) Bluse ist zu (**18** teuer) und das (**19** elegant) Kleid macht sie zu (**20** alt). Sie fühlt sich (**21** wohl) in ihren (**22** alt) Jeans. Wenn sie nach England kommt, wird sie sich etwas (**23** neu) kaufen.

C)> The following is based on an extract from a tourist brochure produced by the Hilton Hotel in Weimar. Again, the adjectives are left for you to complete.

Die Stadt Weimar ist über 1000 Jahre (**1** alt). (**2** Lang) Zeit spielte sie die (**3** führend) Rolle in der (**4** deutsch) Geistesgeschichte. Zu Beginn des 19. Jahrhunderts lebte hier der (**5** größt) deutsche Dichter, Johann Wolfgang von Goethe. Und hier tagte auch die (**6** deutsch) Nationalversammlung nach der Beendigung des (**7** Erst) Weltkrieges, um eine (**8** neu) Verfassung zu beschließen, nämlich die Verfassung der (**9** Weimar) Republik.

Die (**10** mittelalterlich) Straßen Weimars mit ihren (**11** malerisch) Häusern haben sich kaum verändert.

Ganz in der Nähe von Weimar beginnt der (**12** Thüringen) Wald, eine der (**13** schönst) und (**14** unverdorbenst) Naturregionen Europas. Wanderwege führen Sie kilometerweit durch die (**15** ausgedehnt) Wälder dieser Berglandschaft, vorbei an (**16** sprudelnd) Wildwasserbächen und (**17** blühend) Wiesen.

Making longer statements

Frauen lernen ein Handwerk

Studium, Lehre oder Arbeit?

Dieter, Roswitha und Susan sitzen in einer Kneipe **und**   11.1
unterhalten sich über Weiterbildung und über die Gleich-
berechtigung von Mann und Frau.

Roswitha   Ich habe irgendwo gelesen, **dass ihr Briten**   11.2
euch viel mehr für die Weiterbildung interes-
siert als wir. Jeder zehnte Brite sagte in
einer Umfrage, dass er in den letzten vier
Wochen an einer Weiterbildung teilgenommen
hat. In Deutschland war es zu gleicher Zeit
nur jeder dreißigste Befragte. Das sind sehr
viele bei euch, **die sich weiterbilden wollen**.   11.3
Stimmt das?

Susan	Ich weiss nicht, **aber es kann schon stimmen.**	11.1
	Viele Leute melden sich jedes Jahr für eine	
	Weiterbildung. Aber die Schwierigkeiten findet	
	man erst später. Viele, **die einen Kurs beginnen,**	11.3
	geben schnell auf, **weil es zu schwer ist.**	11.2
Roswitha	Da hast du Recht. **Wenn etwas schwer ist, gibt**	11.5
	man schnell auf. Ich habe mein Studium auch	
	oft aufgeben wollen, **aber ich studiere gern.** Man	11.1
	lernt immer etwas Neues, **weil man hofft, dass**	11.2
	es auf längere Sicht **zu einer guten Position führt.**	11.2
	Und du, Dieter? Hast du auch manchmal	
	Zweifel gehabt?	
Dieter	Natürlich. Manchmal denkt man, warum	
	studieren? Einen Beruf lernen hat doch große	
	Vorteile, **denn man lernt und arbeitet gleichzeitig**	11.1
	und verdient Geld.	
Roswitha	Dein Bruder hat wohl auch viel Praktisches	
	gelernt, **seitdem er bei der Post arbeitet.**	11.2
Dieter	Ja, und für ihn war das die beste Lösung. Er hat	
	schon früh Geld verdient, hat etwas Positives	
	getan **und kann trotzdem nun studieren, weil**	11.1 / 11.2
	ihn das jetzt mehr interessiert.	
Susan	Es muss ja nicht jeder studieren. Auch als Frau	
	hat man die Wahl. Weisst du, **wie viele Frauen**	11.4
	ein Handwerk lernen?	
Dieter	Das weiß ich nicht, aber ich weiß, **dass es** bei	11.2
	Lucas in Koblenz **ein Projekt gibt**, nämlich	
	„Women in Lucas", **das für Chancengleichheit**	11.3
	von Männern und Frauen sorgen soll. Du siehst,	
	es wird etwas für die Gleichberechtigung getan.	
Roswitha	Lucas ist aber eine englische Firma. Weißt du,	
	ob es solche Projekte auch bei deutschen	11.4
	Firmen gibt?	
Dieter	Die gibt es sicherlich. Aber im Detail kann ich	
	das nicht sagen. **Dass Lucas dieses Programm**	11.5
	hat, habe ich zufällig in der Zeitung gelesen.	
Roswitha	Man soll nicht **alles** glauben, **was man in der**	11.3
	Zeitung liest!	

11.1 Second main clauses

und unterhalten sich
aber ich studiere gern
aber es kann schon stimmen
denn man lernt und arbeitet gleichzeitig
und kann trotzdem nun studieren

○ Every sentence must contain at least one *finite verb*. By finite verb we mean a verb which changes according to the subject; this is the verb which takes the first verb position (see section 6.1). As you already know, there can be second verbs which go to the final verb position. For example, in the sentence:

> Ich kann morgen nach London fahren.

kann is the finite verb and **fahren** is an infinitive dependent on it.

○ But a longer sentence can have two or more finite verbs. In order to talk about such sentences, we use the word *clause* to mean any part of a sentence which has its own finite verb. So in:

> Ich fahre nach London und meine Freundin fährt nach Birmingham.

the finite verbs are clearly **fahre** and **fährt**, and the two clauses are:

> Ich fahre nach London
> und meine Freundin fährt nach Birmingham.

○ Where (as in the above example), the two clauses are equally important, we can speak of the second as being a *second main clause*.

Clauses other than the first main clause are introduced by *conjunctions*. German conjunctions which can introduce second main clauses are:

aber	*but*
denn	*for, since, because*
oder	*or*
sondern	*but* (after a negative)
und	*and*

e.g. aber ich studiere gern
but I like studying

denn man lernt und arbeitet gleichzeitig
because you learn and work at the same time

Second main clauses pose few problems because the word order is the same as in a first main clause.

○ Two or more clauses in a sentence are usually separated in German by a comma.

e.g. Ich habe mein Studium oft aufgeben wollen, aber ich studiere gern.
I have often wanted to give up my studies, but I like studying.

Einen Beruf lernen hat große Vorteile, denn man arbeitet praktisch.
Learning a trade has great advantages, because you do practical work.

Er kommt nicht mit, sondern er fährt nach Berlin.
He's not coming with us, he's going to Berlin.

However, there is an important exception. Since the German spelling reform, it is now optional whether to insert a comma before **und** or **oder**. The comma need only be inserted if the writer believes it will make the meaning clearer.

e.g. Roswitha und Susan unterhalten sich und Dieter hört zu.
Roswitha and Susan are chatting and Dieter just listens.

Here there is no need for a comma. But if the sentence was:

Roswitha unterhält sich mit Susan, und Dieter hört zu.
Roswitha chats to Susan, and Dieter just listens.

the comma is useful so that the reader does not at first read it as **unterhält sich mit Susan und Dieter**.

》 Combine the following pairs of sentences with 'und', 'aber', 'oder', 'sondern' or 'denn'.

e.g. Carla kommt aus Deutschland. Susan kommt aus England.
Carla kommt aus Deutschland, aber Susan kommt aus England.

1 Carla kommt nicht aus England. Sie kommt aus Deutschland.
2 Meistens trinke ich Tee. Manchmal trinke ich Kaffee.
3 Ich kann das Kleid nicht kaufen. Ich habe kein Geld.

4   Dieter geht zu Fuß. Er hat kein Auto.
5   Sie sind nicht ins Kino gegangen. Sie haben einen
     Spaziergang gemacht.
6   Trinken Sie ein Glas Bier? Möchten Sie eine Tasse Kaffee?
7   Er ist mit dem Taxi gefahren. Er hatte keine Zeit.
8   Ich habe eine Fahrkarte gekauft. Ich bin nach München
     gefahren.
9   Jeder möchte gern lernen. Jeder möchte beruflich
     weiterkommen.
10   Mein Bruder hat einen praktischen Beruf gelernt. Jetzt möchte
     er studieren.

11.2 Subordinate clauses

dass ihr Briten euch mehr für die Weiterbildung interessiert
weil man hofft
weil es zu schwer ist
dass es ein Projekt gibt
dass es zu einer guten Position führt
weil ihn das jetzt mehr interessiert
seitdem er bei der Post arbeitet

O   Not all clauses are main clauses. Sometimes a clause will convey
    information which is dependent on that of a main clause to make
    sense. Such clauses are called **subordinate clauses**. Subordinate
    clauses cannot stand on their own (unless the main clause is
    implied but not actually spoken or written).

O   German conjunctions which introduce subordinate clauses include:

als	*when* (in the past)
als ob	*as if*
bevor	*before*
da	*since* (= *because*)
dass	*that*
ob	*whether*
seitdem	*since* (*in time*)
wenn	*if, when* (present or future or in past as *whenever*)
weil	*because*

○ In a subordinate clause, the finite verb goes to the very end of the clause.

e.g. weil es zu schwer **ist**
because it is too difficult

dass es zu einer guten Position **führt**
that it will lead to a good job

dass es ein Projekt **gibt**
that there is a project

In a single sentence there can be more than one subordinate clause.

e.g. weil man **hofft**, dass es zu einer guten Position **führt**
because you hope that it will lead to a good job

○ If there is an infinitive or participle as well as the finite verb in the clause, the finite verb will go after it.

e.g. Ich möchte nach Berlin fahren.
weil ich nach Berlin fahren möchte
Er hat Chemie studiert.
weil er Chemie studiert hat

○ The subject of the subordinate clause almost always follows straight after the conjunction.

e.g. Morgen abend kommt Peter.
Ich weiß, dass **Peter** morgen abend kommt.

○ Note that after **seitdem** (which can often be shortened to **seit**), German uses the present tense if the action is still going on.

e.g. Seit(dem) er bei der Post arbeitet...
Since he has been working for the Post Office...

(For the use of **seit** in single-clause sentence, see section 4.7.)

A)⟩ In section 1.2, we learnt a little about Carla's daily routine. Take the following statements and rephrase them starting with 'Wir wissen schon, dass ...'

e.g. Ich gehe jeden Tag zu Fuß zur Schule.
Wir wissen schon, dass sie jeden Tag zu Fuß zur Schule geht.

1 Die Schule ist nicht weit vom Haus.
2 Die erste Stunde beginnt um 7.50 Uhr.
3 Nachmittags mache ich Schulaufgaben.
4 Ich besuche später eine Freundin.
5 Wir hören Musik.
6 Abends bleibe ich meistens zu Hause.
7 Ich schreibe selten Briefe.

B)⟩ Link the following sentences together using 'weil'.

e.g. Ich fahre nach Deutschland. Ich will Deutsch lernen.
Ich fahre nach Deutschland, weil ich Deutsch lernen will.

1 Wir kaufen dieses Kleid. Es ist billig.
2 Roswitha lernt viel. Sie möchte ein gutes Examen machen.
3 Wir können nicht ausgehen. Wir haben kein Geld.
4 Roswitha bewirbt sich um eine Stelle. Sie sucht einen Arbeitsplatz.
5 Dieters Bruder studiert. Er möchte seine Berufsaussichten verbessern.
6 Ich trinke viel Limonade. Es ist sehr heiß.
7 Roswitha fährt nach Alzey. Sie möchte ihre Eltern besuchen.
8 Dieter weiß vom Projekt bei Lucas. Er hat es in der Zeitung gelesen.
9 Dieter liest die Zeitung. Er möchte sich informieren.
10 Hans geht zu Fuß. Das Auto ist in der Werkstatt.

11.3 Relative clauses

die sich weiterbilden wollen
die einen Kurs beginnen
das für Chancengleichheit sorgen soll
alles, was man in der Zeitung liest

○ A *relative clause* is a subordinate clause which relates to a specific item in the main clause. It is introduced by a *relative pronoun* (equivalent to the English *who* or *which*). In the sentence:

That is the man who works in Frankfurt.

the clause *who works in Frankfurt* is a relative clause relating to *man*. Similarly, in:

Those are the books which we bought yesterday.

which we bought yesterday is a relative clause relating to *books*.

○ German does not distinguish between *who* and *which*. The German relative pronouns are similar to the definite article, i.e.

	Masculine	*Neuter*	*Feminine*	*Plural*
Nominative	der	das	die	die
Accusative	den	das	die	die
Dative	dem	dem	der	**denen**
Genitive	**dessen**	**dessen**	**deren**	**deren**

○ The gender of the relative pronoun will depend upon the noun to which it relates. Its case will depend on its function in the relative clause.

e.g. Der Mann, **der** in Frankfurt arbeitet.   (nom.)
The man who works in Frankfurt.

Der Mann, **den** ich gestern gesehen habe.   (acc.)
The man whom I saw yesterday.

Der Mann, von **dem** ich dir erzählt habe.   (dat.)
The man of whom I told you.

Der Mann, **dessen** Tochter ich kenne.   (gen.)
The man whose daughter I know.

Two points to note:

a) In the genitive, the gender of the **dessen** or **deren** depends on the 'owner'. So in the final example on page 175, **dessen** is used because it refers back to **der Mann**. The gender of **die Tochter** makes no difference.

b) Unlike English, German cannot omit the relative pronoun. In the second and third of the examples on page 175, English could say:

> *The man I saw yesterday.*
> and *The man I told you about.*

German has to use the full relative clause including the relative pronoun.

○ As in other subordinate clauses, the finite verb is at the end and the clause is separated off by a comma.

> viele Leute, die sich weiterbilden wollen
> *a lot of people who want to do further training*

> ein Projekt, das für Chancengleichheit sorgen soll
> *a project that is supposed to promote equal opportunities*

○ Be careful to distinguish between the relative pronoun **das** and the conjunction **dass**. The pronoun relates to something specific in the main clause; the conjunction serves only to introduce the new clause.

○ **was** is used as a relative pronoun if the main clause includes **alles**, **etwas**, **nichts** or an indefinite **das** (i.e. where the **das** is a general *that* rather than referring to a specific neuter noun).

> Er hat genau das, was wir suchen.
> *He has just what we are looking for.*

> Alles, was man in der Zeitung liest.
> *Everything that you read in the newspaper.*

○ An increasingly common construction is a relative clause preceded by **derjenige, diejenige, dasjenige** or plural **diejenigen** meaning *the one who, the ones who*:

> diejenigen, die einen Kurs beginnen
> *those who begin a course*

A⟩⟩ Susan has drawn up a list of the presents she has bought, and explains it to Roswitha. Then Roswitha repeats the same information to Dieter. But where Susan used two short sentences for each item, Roswitha only uses one.

e.g. Das Buch ist für meinen Bruder. Er studiert Geschichte.
Das Buch ist für ihren Bruder, der Geschichte studiert.

1 Die Bluse ist für meine Schwester. Sie geht noch zur Schule.
2 Die Flasche ist für meinen Vater. Er trinkt gern Wein.
3 Der Schal ist für meine Oma. Sie ist fünfundsiebzig.
4 Die Zigarren sind für meinen Onkel. Er raucht gern.
5 Die Schokolade ist für meine kleine Schwester. Sie isst alles Süße.
6 Die Krawatte ist für meinen Vetter. Er wohnt in Leicester.
7 Der Teller ist für meine Freundin. Sie konnte nicht nach Deutschland fahren.
8 Das Plakat ist für die Deutschlehrerin. Sie ist sehr nett.
9 Das Kuchenrezept ist für meine Mutter. Sie bäckt gern Kuchen.
10 Der Bierkrug ist für meinen Freund. Er holt mich von der Schule ab.

B⟩⟩ In the following statements about the relatives in Alzey, complete the relative pronouns.

1 Elfriede und Karl, _____ in Alzey wohnen, haben ein Weingut.
2 Die Großmutter, _____ bei Elfriede und Karl wohnt, arbeitet noch eifrig mit.
3 Auf dem Weingut, _____ nicht sehr groß ist, wachsen verschiedene Reben.
4 Hans, _____ der Bruder von Elfriede ist, arbeitet in Frankfurt und wohnt in Usingen.
5 Die Reben, _____ sie im Herbst in großen Körbern ernten, werden zur Presse gefahren.
6 Der Traktor, auf _____ die Reben transportiert werden, ist nicht sehr groß.
7 Roswitha, _____ Familie noch immer in Alzey wohnt, kommt oft nach Hause.
8 Karl, _____ Schwiegermutter Geburtstag feiert, ist Winzer.
9 Die Oma, zu _____ Geburtstag die jungen Leute fahren, erzählt viel von der guten alten Zeit.
10 Der Wein, _____ die Kommission prüft, wird mit einem Prädikat ausgezeichnet.

177

C⟩⟩ Integrate the information in brackets by means of a relative clause.

e.g. Der Student kommt aus Sachsen. (Er wohnt in diesem Zimmer)
Der Student, der in diesem Zimmer wohnt, kommt aus Sachsen.

1 Das Geld ist für die Miete. (Es liegt auf dem Tisch)
2 Die Studenten warten auf die Straßenbahn. (Sie stehen an der Haltestelle)
3 Der Computer ist sehr modern. (Roswitha hat ihn gekauft)
4 Die Stereoanlage ist sehr teuer. (Ich habe sie in einem Schaufenster gesehen)
5 Die Wirtin ist sehr nett. (Roswitha wohnt bei ihr)
6 Der Mann tut mir leid. (Seine Frau ist krank)
7 Der Student ruft die Werkstatt an. (Sein Auto ist kaputt)
8 Meine Freunde wohnen in München. (Ich habe ihnen gestern geschrieben)
9 Die Bücher sind sehr interessant. (Ich habe sie mir geliehen)
10 Die Engländerin war sehr nett. (Sie war bei unseren Freunden)

Die Studenten warten auf die Straßenbahn

11.4 Indirect questions

> wie viele Frauen ein Handwerk lernen
> ob es solche Projekte auch bei deutschen Firmen gibt

○ A subordinate clause may also be adapted from a question. This is particularly the case when you are talking about what somebody knows or doesn't know. The sentence:

> *I don't know how many women learn a trade.*

is based on the original question:

> *How many women learn a trade?*

In German, because the original question has now become a subordinate clause, it is of course separated by a comma, and the verb is at the end.

> Ich weiß nicht, wie viele Frauen ein Handwerk lernen.

Where the original question is one which starts with the verb, as in:

> Gibt es solche Projekte auch bei deutschen Firmen?
> *Do similar projects exist in German companies as well?*

a new conjunction is required when the question is integrated into a longer sentence. The conjunction **ob** (*whether*) is used for this purpose:

> Weißt du, **ob** es solche Projekte auch bei deutschen Firmen gibt?
> Ich weiß nicht, **ob** es solche Projekte auch bei deutschen Firmen gibt.

》 Imagine that you are being asked a lot of questions to which you do not know the answer. In each case, start your reply with 'Ich weiß nicht ...'

e.g. Hat Susan einen Freund?
　　　 Ich weiß nicht, ob sie einen Freund hat.

1　Hat Hans eine Freundin?
2　Wann beginnt der Film?
3　Ist das eine positive Entwicklung?
4　Wie hoch ist die Zugspitze?

> **5** Wie alt ist Roswitha?
> **6** Hat sie Geschwister?
> **7** Wie lange studiert sie schon?
> **8** Was möchte Dieter später werden?
> **9** Haben Roswithas Eltern auch studiert?
> **10** Wann wird Roswitha fertig?

11.5 Starting with a subordinate clause

> Wenn etwas schwer ist, gibt man schnell auf.
> Dass Lucas dieses Programm hat, habe ich in der Zeitung
> gelesen.

○ Very frequently, a subordinate clause is used to start the sentence. In this case, it must be followed immediately by the verb from the main clause.

e.g. Man gibt schnell auf, wenn etwas zu schwer ist.
You soon give up if something is too difficult.

becomes

Wenn etwas zu schwer ist, **gibt** man schnell auf.

Similarly:

Dass Lucas dieses Programm hat, **habe** ich in der Zeitung gelesen.
That Lucas has this project is something I read in the paper.

≫ Rewrite the following, starting with the subordinate clause:

e.g. Dieters Bruder möchte studieren, weil er bessere Berufsaussichten sucht.
Weil Dieters Bruder bessere Berufsaussichten sucht, möchte er studieren.

1 Dieter geht mit Roswitha in die Kneipe, obwohl er nicht viel Zeit hat.
2 Susan ruft ihre Eltern an, nachdem sie gegessen hat.

3   Die Studenten fahren nach Bad Dürkheim, weil der
    Wurstmarkt sehr bekannt ist.
4   Ich lernte Fahrrad fahren, als ich acht Jahre alt war.
5   Ich fuhr zum ersten Mal nach Deutschland, als ich 17 Jahre alt
    war.
6   Dieter liest viele Zeitungen, weil er sich informieren will.
7   Susan kauft die weiße Bluse nicht, weil sie so teuer ist.
8   In der Zeitung stand, dass jeder zehnte Brite eine
    Weiterbildung gemacht hat.
9   Ich trinke viel Limonade, wenn es sehr heiß ist.
10 Ich habe schon in der Zeitung gelesen, dass es ein neues
    Projekt gibt.

Ich trinke viel Limonade, wenn es sehr heiß ist

12 Relating who said what

*Es wurde berichtet, die Einwohner
hätten dagegen demonstriert*

Die neue Klinik

Dieter hat wieder einen interessanten Zeitungsartikel gefunden, diesmal
über den Bau einer neuen Klinik in Schilda, einem Ort,
der von Bergen und Wäldern umgeben ist. Der Bau dieser
Klinik ist sehr umstritten und wird in der Presse stark diskutiert.

Roswitha	Man sagt, **der Stadtrat hätte die Genehmigung** für den Bau der Klinik auf dem Berg **gegeben**.	12.3
Dieter	Ja, hier zitiert man den Chefarzt. „Wegen der gesunden Lage der Klinik mitten im Wald **erhoffe man einen großen Andrang** von Patienten. Nicht nur Patienten aus Deutschland sondern aus der ganzen Welt **seien zu erwarten. Die Klinik solle auch viele Arbeitsplätze** für die Einwohner von Schilda und den Nachbardörfern **schaffen**. Er fragte, **wo man sonst eine so schöne Klinik bauen könne**."	12.2 12.2 12.2 12.4

Roswitha	Du kannst aufhören mit dem Vorlesen. Ich kann mir gut vorstellen, wie das weitergeht. „Um die Klinik **gebe** es Spazierwege, damit **hätten Patienten die Gelegenheit**, in der frischen Luft spazieren zu gehen." Und damit ruinieren sie das Bild des Berges. Warst du schon einmal da? Es ist landschaftlich sehr schön.

12.2 / 12.3

Hans	Aber es gibt doch keine Alternative.
Roswitha	Natürlich gibt es eine Alternative. Die Bürgerinitiative Schilda hat schon den Vorschlag gemacht, **Kliniken müssten dort gebaut werden, wo es schon Straßen gäbe**.

12.3

Hans	Aber wo soll man die Klinik bauen? Sie soll in einer schönen Umgebung liegen, damit die Leute in gesunder Umgebung sich wohlfühlen können.
Roswitha	Mich regt auf, wieviel Geld für die Rodung des Waldes ausgegeben wird. Man könnte bestimmt einen anderen Platz finden. Es wird auch gesagt, **dass der Staat einen Zuschuss** von mehreren Millionen Mark **bewilligt hat**.

12.1

Hans	Wer sagt das? Wo hast du die Zahlen her? So ein Klinikbau kostet immer viel. Auch du brauchst mal eine Klinik, wenn du krank bist.
Roswitha	Aber nicht mitten im Wald. Auf der einen Seite wird gesagt, **man solle die Umwelt schonen** und auf der anderen Seite wird ein großer Eingriff in die Natur genehmigt.

12.4

Dieter	Roswitha hat Recht. Es wäre möglich eine schöne Klinik in Sonnental zu bauen, das ist schon teilweise bebaut und nicht weit vom Wald. Aber es wurde berichtet, **die Einwohner hätten dagegen demonstriert**. Sie **würden befürchten**, dass ein Klinikbau **schwerwiegende Konsequenzen** für den Wohnwert der Gegend **hätte**.

12.3
12.3
12.3

12.1 Indirect speech with *dass*

...dass der Staat einen Zuschuss bewilligt hat

When we repeat what somebody else says, we can either quote them word for word, or we can use **indirect speech**. We can say either:

> *He says, 'I am tired'* (direct quote)
> or   *He says (that) he is tired* (indirect speech).

Indirect speech is more usual.

○ German also has a choice between a direct quote and indirect speech, and also prefers indirect speech. In spoken German, and increasingly in written German, all that is necessary is to make the indirect speech a subordinate clause introduced by the conjunction **dass**.

> Er sagt, dass er müde ist.

OR as in our dialogue:

> Es wird auch gesagt, dass der Staat einen Zuschuss bewilligt hat.
> *It is also said that the state has agreed a subsidy.*

○ In both English and German, if the 'reporter' is different from the original speaker, and the original speaker uses the 1st person (*I/we*), this has to be changed to the 3rd person (*he/she/they*) in the indirect speech.

> *Dieter: 'I am tired'.*
> *Dieter says that **he** is tired.*
> Dieter sagt, dass **er** müde ist.

Also in both languages, if the original speech is some time in the past, you may need to change the tense to show that things have or may have changed.

> *Dieter **said** that he **is** tired (and he probably still is).*
> Dieter **sagte,** dass er müde **ist.**

> *Dieter **said** that he **was** tired (when he spoke, but that was last week).*
> Dieter **sagte,** dass er müde **war.**

>> The following are statements Roswitha makes about the new clinic. Rewrite them, starting with 'Sie sagt, dass ...'

e.g. Ein Bus soll von der Stadt zur Klinik fahren.
       Sie sagt, dass ein Bus von der Stadt zur Klinik fahren soll.

1 Man muss den Wald roden.
2 Das Tierleben wird gefährdet.
3 Die neue Straße führt direkt über den Wildpfad von Hirschen und Rehen.
4 Der Staat hat einen Zuschuss bewilligt.
5 Die Besiedlung des Berges verunreinigt das Wasser der Mineralquelle.

12.2 Subjunctive 1 in indirect speech

man erhoffe einen großen Andrang
Patienten aus der ganzen Welt seien zu erwarten.
Die Klinik solle viele Arbeitsplätze schaffen.
es gebe Spazierwege

○ There is another technique that is frequently used in written German, especially in newspapers, and is regarded as the most elegant way of reporting speech. There is no need for the **dass**, the word order of the original speaker is retained but the verb takes a form known as *subjunctive 1*.

Er sagte, er **habe** kein Geld.

The forms of subjunctive 1 for a regular verb are:

	Present	Subjunctive 1
ich	kaufe	kaufe
du	kaufst	kauf**est**
er/sie/es	kauft	kauf**e**
wir/sie/Sie	kaufen	kaufen
ihr	kauft	kauf**et**

185

○ But you can only omit the **dass** if the subjunctive 1 form is different from the present tense. As you will see from the example on page 185, this applies only in the **du**, **er/sie/es** and **ihr** forms. It is the **-e** ending on the 3rd person singular (**er/sie/es**) which is characteristic of subjunctive 1 and is most frequently used in indirect speech.

Some more examples of the 3rd person singular of subjunctive 1:

Infinitive	Subjunctive 1
kommen	er/sie/es komme
geben	er/sie/es gebe
haben	er/sie/es habe
können	er/sie/es könne
werden	er/sie/es werde

e.g. Um die Klinik **gebe** es Spazierwege.
(*He said that*) *around the clinic there were paths.*

○ Where the subjunctive 1 form is different from the present tense, you also do not need to say, let alone to keep repeating, *he said that ..., he indicated that ...* etc.

e.g. Man erhoffe einen großen Andrang.
(*The senior consultant said that*) *they were hoping for a big demand.*

Die Klinik solle viele Arbeitsplätze schaffen.
(*He added that*) *the clinic would create many new jobs.*

○ **sein** is the only verb in which subjunctive 1 differs from the present tense in all its forms:

	Present	Subjunctive 1
ich	bin	**sei**
du	bist	**seist**
er/sie/es	ist	**sei**
wir/sie/Sie	sind	**seien**
ihr	seid	**seiet**

○ The tense in subjunctive 1 reflects the actual words of the speaker.

If the speaker uses the present tense, subjunctive 1 is also used in the present.

> Er sagte: „Ich kaufe ein Auto"
> Er sagte, er kaufe ein Auto.
> *He said he is/was buying a car.*

But if he/she used the past tense, then the reporter uses subjunctive 1 in the perfect, i.e. subjunctive 1 of **haben** or **sein** as appropriate plus the past participle.

> Er sagte: „Ich kaufte im Januar ein Auto".
> Er sagte, er habe im Januar ein Auto gekauft.

A⟩⟩ Imagine that a newspaper reporter is writing about local people's views on the new clinic, and wishes to report what Roswitha has said. Take her statements from the exercise at the top of page 185, and rewrite them for the newspaper using subjunctive 1.

e.g. Ein Bus soll von der Stadt zur Klinik fahren.
Ein Bus **solle** von der Stadt zur Klinik fahren.

B⟩⟩ The following is a newspaper report of an accident. Write out the exact words the cyclist will have used when speaking to the reporter. Start: 'Ich war auf der Vorfahrtsstraße ...'

Gestern abend ereignete sich ein Unfall in der Rolandstraße. Ein Radfahrer wurde leicht verletzt. Unserem Berichterstatter erzählte der Radfahrer später, er sei auf der Vorfahrtstraße gewesen. Plötzlich sei ein Auto aus der Seitenstraße gekommen. Es könne nicht gehalten haben, denn es sei zu schnell aus der Seitenstraße gekommen. Er habe geschrien und auf die Bremse getreten, aber trotzdem sei er auf das Auto geprallt. Dann habe er auf der Straße gelegen. Der Autofahrer habe mitten auf der Straße angehalten. Der Radfahrer habe unter Schock gestanden und habe versucht, aufzustehen. Das Fahrrad sei kaputt gewesen, das Auto habe nur Blechschaden erlitten.

12.3 Subjunctive 2 in indirect speech

Der Stadtrat hätte die Genehmigung gegeben.
damit hätten Patienten die Gelegenheit
Kliniken müssten dort gebaut werden, wo es schon Straßen gäbe.
Die Einwohner hätten dagegen protestiert.
sie würden befürchten
Ein Klinikbau hätte schwerwiegende Konsequenzen.

○ Where subjunctive 1 is the same as the present tense, it cannot be used to indicate indirect speech. Subjunctive 2 is used instead.

As outlined in section 8.4, subjunctive 2 is formed from the simple past tense, with the addition of the endings **-e, -est, -e, -en, -et**. Where the simple past contains **a, o** or **u**, an umlaut is usually added.

As you will see from the following examples, this means that in the case of weak verbs, subjunctive 2 is identical with the simple past. But with strong verbs, there are important differences, especially when an umlaut is added:

	Simple past	*Subjunctive 2*
Weak verb: kaufen		
ich	kaufte	kaufte
du	kauftest	kauftest
er/sie/es	kaufte	kaufte
wir/Sie/sie	kauften	kauften
ihr	kauftet	kauftet
Strong verb without umlaut: gehen		
ich	ging	ging**e**
du	gingst	ging**est**
er/sie/es	ging	ging**e**
wir	gingen	gingen
ihr	gingt	ging**et**

	Simple past	Subjunctive 2
Strong verb with umlaut: singen		
ich	sang	s**ä**ng**e**
du	sangst	s**ä**ng**est**
er/sie/es	sang	s**ä**ng**e**
wir/Sie/sie	sangen	s**ä**ngen
ihr	sangt	s**ä**ng**et**

O   Some more examples of subjunctive 2 with strong verbs:

	ich er/sie/es	du	wir/Sie/sie	ihr
kommen	käme	kämest	kämen	kämet
finden	fände	fändest	fänden	fändet
fahren	führe	führest	führen	führet

You will find a list of the most commonly used Subjunctive 2 forms on page 129, and can work out more from the list of strong and mixed verbs on pages 112-113.

Some examples from the dialogue:

> die Einwohner **hätten** dagegen protestiert
> *the locals had demonstrated against it*

> damit **hätten** Patienten die Gelegenheit
> *so patients would have the opportunity*

> Kliniken **müssten** dort gebaut werden
> *clinics ought to be built*

(In all three cases, the subjunctive 1 forms **haben** and **müssen** would be identical with the present tense.)

O   In spoken German, subjunctive 2 is also preferred for another reason, i.e. because subjunctive 1 sounds rather stilted and affected. When Roswitha is chatting to her friends and telling them what other people have said, she uses subjunctive 2 to say:

> Man sagt, der Stadtrat hätte die Genehmigung gegeben.
> *They say the council has given approval.*

(Kliniken müssten dort gebaut werden) wo es schon
Straßen gäbe.
(Clinics should be built) where there are already roads.

Had she been quoting these views in an article for a newspaper, she
would have used subjunctive 1 forms **habe** and **gebe** . But this
would sound unnatural in colloquial German.

○ If neither subjunctive 1 nor subjunctive 2 is sufficiently distinctive
to indicate indirect speech, you can use **würde** (subjunctive 2 of
werden) plus the infinitive:

Sie würden befürchten ...
(It was reported that) they were afraid ...

○ Many Germans are totally confused by the subjunctive and use
subjunctive 1, subjunctive 2 and the present or perfect all mixed up
together. The language is evolving, and it is not currently possible to
give precise rules. The following guidelines should help:

a) Always choose a subjunctive form that is distinctly different
from the present tense. This makes it clear that you are quoting
from somebody else, and you can avoid clumsy word order.

b) Where subjunctive 1 has a different form from the present
tense, use it for reported speech. If subjunctive 1 is the same
as the present tense, use subjunctive 2.

c) Especially in spoken (rather than written) German, remember
the alternatives:

dass ... and the present or simple past as appropriate
würde plus the infinitive.

» In the following reports of what people have said, reconstruct the
original words.

e.g. Elfriede sagte, sie hätten dieses Jahr eine gute Ernte gehabt.
Elfriede sagte: „Wir haben dieses Jahr eine gute Ernte gehabt".

1 Roswitha und Susan haben gesagt, sie würden einkaufen gehen.
2 Herr Schulz hat gesagt, er komme aus Sachsen und habe in
Berlin studiert. Jetzt wohne er in Frankfurt. Er unterrichte
Mathematik dort. Sein Bruder und seine Schwester würden in
Leipzig wohnen, aber sie kämen oft nach Frankfurt.

3   Der Chefarzt behauptete, der Berg sei die idealste Lage für die
    Klinik. Er habe in einer ähnlichen Klinik in Österreich gearbeitet;
    dort seien die Patienten aus aller Welt sehr zufrieden gewesen.
    Die gute Luft und die Möglichkeit, Spaziergänge zu
    unternehmen, würden die Genesung der Patienten
    beschleunigen.

12.4 Questions and requests in indirect speech

Er fragte, wo man sonst eine Klinik bauen könne.
Es wird gesagt, man solle die Umwelt schonen.

○   Where indirect speech includes a question, the same pattern
    applies as for statements. Subjunctive 1 is regarded as the more
    elegant, with subjunctive 2 used when subjunctive 1 is the same
    as the present.

So: Wo kann man sonst eine so schöne Klinik bauen?
      Where else can one build such a fine clinic?

becomes:

      Er fragte, wo man sonst eine so schöne Klinik bauen könne.
      He asked where else one could build such a fine clinic.

○   Where the original speaker has used an imperative for a request,
    the reporter will need to use a modal verb, usually *sollen:*

      Schonen wir die Umwelt!
      Let's spare the environment!

becomes:

      Es wird gesagt, man solle die Umwelt schonen.
      It is said that one should spare the environment.

> Rufen Sie mich morgen im Büro an!
> *Phone me in the office tomorrow.*

becomes:

> Der Chef sagte, man solle ihn morgen im Büro anrufen.
> *The boss said one should phone him in the office tomorrow.*

Note that you cannot use a simple infinitive in German for indirect commands. For the previous example, it is possible in English to say:

> *The boss told them to phone him in the office tomorrow.*

German has to make a separate clause out of the request.
(Exception: **bitten,** used with **zu** + infinitive:

> Der Chef bat sie, ihn morgen im Büro anzurufen.
> *The boss asked them to phone him in the office tomorrow*).

>> A manager is going on holiday, and leaves the following instructions on his dictating machine. His secretary, Frau Müller, reads out a summary. Can you reconstruct the original message?

e.g. Herrr Görner soll bitte die Besprechung vorbereiten.
      „Herr Görner, bitte bereiten Sie die Besprechung vor."

1   Frau Meyer soll bitte die Hotelzimmer reservieren.
2   Herr Reinhard soll bitte die Briefe unterschreiben.
3   Ich soll die Post aufmachen.
4   Frau Neumann soll die Akten einordnen.
5   Frau Wilhelm soll bitte die Rechnungen sortieren..

Ich soll die Post aufmachen

Answer section

Unit 1

1.1

A   1 er 2 sie 3 sie

B   1 wir 2 du 3 ich 4 ihr 5 Sie

1.2

A   gehe ist beginnt komme ist mache geht besuche sitzen
plaudern hören erzählen planen bleibe gehe spüle schreibe

B   Sie geht jeden Tag zu Fuß zur Schule. Die Schule ist nicht weit
vom Haus. Die erste Stunde beginnt um 7.50 Uhr. Meist kommt sie sogar
pünktlich! Mittags um 13.00 Uhr ist die Schule zu Ende. Nachmittags macht
sie Schulaufgaben. Das geht sehr schnell. Meist besucht sie etwas später
eine Freundin. Sie sitzen zusammen, plaudern, hören Musik, erzählen von
Freunden und planen etwas für das Wochenende. Abends bleibt sie
meistens zu Hause, aber manchmal geht sie aus. Ganz selten spült sie das
Geschirr oder schreibt Briefe.

C   1 Wo wohnst du?
2 Gehst du noch zur Schule?
3 Kommst du oft in die Disko?
4 Wie lange kennst du schon Carla?

1.3

A   1 ich lese du liest er/sie/es liest wir/Sie/sie lesen ihr lest
2 ich fahre du fährst er/sie/es fährt wir/Sie/sie fahren ihr fahrt
3 ich arbeite du arbeitest er/sie/es arbeitet wir/Sie/sie arbeiten
ihr arbeitet

B   1 Sie fährt ...   2 Sie bastelt ...   3 Sie sammelt ...   4 Sie arbeitet ...
5 Sie schreibt ...

C   Er kommt aus Usingen und arbeitet als Computerprogrammierer
in Frankfurt. Er spricht etwas Englisch, in der Computerindustrie sprechen
sie fast alle Englisch. Er findet die Arbeit sehr interessant. Er treibt viel
Sport, besonders Leichtathletik und läuft 100 m.

1.4

A   1 bin   2 ist   3 ist   4 bist   5 sind   6 seid   7 sind   8 ist

B   1 habe   2 hast hat hat   3 hat   4 haben haben habt   5 haben

1.5   **1** gib **2** komm **3** tanz **4** geht **5** singt
6 schreib **7** nehmen **8** sagen **9** hol schlag

1.6   **1** Ja, ich kenne ihn.
2 Ja, ich kenne sie.
3 Ja, ich besuche sie nächste Woche.
4 Ja, ich schicke es nach England.
5 Ja, ich lese sie.
6 Ja, ich schreibe ihn.
7 Ja, ich habe einen Brief für sie.
8 Ja, ich habe ein Geschenk für ihn.
9 Ja, ich schreibe ihn morgen.
10 Ja, ich verstehe dich.
11 Ja, ich sehe euch.

1.7

A   **1** ihr **2** ihnen **3** ihr **4** ihr **5** ihm **6** ihnen **7** ihr

B   **1** Ja, ich helfe Ihnen im Haus.
2 Ja, ich spreche etwas Englisch mit Ihnen.
3 Ja, es geht mir gut.
4 Ja, ich wohne gerne bei Ihnen.
5 Ja, es gefällt mir (gut) hier in Frankfurt.
6 Ja, ich schreibe Ihnen aus England.

C   **1** sie **2** er **3** ihr **4** sie **5** ihn
6 ihnen **7** er ihr **8** ihm **9** ihr **10** ihr

1.8

A   **1** jemand(en) **2** niemand **3** jemand(em) **4** niemand
5 niemand jemand **6** jemand **7** niemand
8 jemand(em) **9** irgendjemand

B   Susan kommt aus Hatfield in der Nähe von London. Sie geht auf eine
Mädchenschule und es gefällt ihr. Sie lernt vier Fächer: Deutsch, Geschichte,
Erdkunde und Englisch. Sie findet Geschichte ganz leicht, aber Deutsch ist
sehr schwer. Sie treibt viel Sport, besonders Leichtathletik. Sie läuft gern
100 m. Samstags geht sie oft mit ihren Freundinnen in die Disko, aber
manchmal fahren sie auch nach London. Sie fährt jetzt nach Frankfurt, aber
sie kennt niemand(en) in Deutschland außer Carla.

Unit 2

2.1   **1** Der Wein ist sehr herb.
2 Meine Arbeit ist abwechslungsreich.

3 Die Stimmung bei der Weinlese ist sehr kameradschaftlich.
4 Viele Leute in der Welt lernen Englisch.
5 Eine englische Studentin und ihr deutscher Freund lernen zusammen Spanisch. Das Lernen macht ihnen Spaß.

2.2

A 1 der Mercedes 2 die Bedienung 3 die Schönheit
4 die Nation 5 der Käfig 6 die Gesellschaft
7 der Idealismus 8 das Skilaufen 9 das Märchen
10 der Mittwoch

B die Arbeit - die Stadt - der Kunde - der Ausschank - der Wein
die Abrechnung - das Finanzamt - der Helfer - die Weinlese
die Weinprobe - der Verkehrsverein - der Besucher - die Welt- die Rebe - die Qualität - der Wein - der Wein - das Weinglas - der Besucher - das Haus

C
1 der Gehalt - content	das Gehalt - salary
2 der Kunde - customer	die Kunde - news
3 der Leiter - manager	die Leiter - ladder
4 der Flur - hall, landing	die Flur - field, pasture
5 der Golf - (geogr.) gulf	das Golf(spiel) - golf
6 der See - inland lake	die See - sea

2.3

A 1 das Rathaus – town hall
2 der Zeitpunkt – (point in) time, moment
3 der Familienbetrieb – family business
4 der Führerschein – driving licence
5 das Wörterbuch – dictionary
6 der Küchenschrank – kitchen cupboard
7 die Automobilindustrie – motor car industry

B 1 unicorn
2 hydrogen
3 lady's bicycle
4 multi-storey car park
5 strawberry
6 boot (of car)
7 antifreeze
8 garden gnome

2.4

A 1 Die Studentinnen studieren in Heidelberg.
2 Die Winzer arbeiten sehr viel.
3 Die Winzerstöchter helfen immer mit.
4 Die Weingüter liegen bei Alzey.

    5 Die Weingläser sind kaputt.
    6 Die Autos fahren sehr schnell.
    7 Die Kunden probieren die Rotweine.

B   **1** mothers – nuts (*as in nuts and bolts*)
    2 banks – benches
    3 ostriches – bunches (*of flowers*)
    4 cockerels – taps
    (*NB Spoken German now uses* Hähne *for both meanings*)

2.5   **1** Er ist Soldat.
    2 Er ist Winzer.
    3 Er ist Pfarrer.
    4 Sie ist Schülerin.
    5 Er ist Bäcker.
    6 Sie ist Lehrerin.

2.6   **1** Die wohnt in Hertfordshire.
    2 Der ist teuer.
    3 Der kann gut tanzen.
    4 Das liegt schön.
    5 Die schmecken sehr gut.

2.7   **1** dieser **2** jede **3** welche **4** dieses
    5 jedes **6** welcher

Unit 3

3.1   **1** Ich habe ein Hemd. Ich habe kein Hemd. Ich habe sechs Hemden.
    2 Ich habe ein Auto. Ich habe kein Auto. Ich habe sechs Autos.
    3 Ich habe ein Radio. Ich habe kein Radio. Ich habe sechs Radios.
    4 Ich habe ein Motorrad. Ich habe kein Motorrad. Ich habe sechs
       Motorräder.
    5 Ich habe eine Flasche Wein. Ich habe keine Flasche Wein. Ich habe
       sechs Flaschen Wein.
    6 Ich habe ein Wörterbuch. Ich habe kein Wörterbuch. Ich habe sechs
       Wörterbücher.
    7 Ich habe eine Jacke. Ich habe keine Jacke. Ich habe sechs Jacken.

3.2   **1** mein **2** dein **3** eure **4** ihr **5** unsere **6** Ihr
    7 meine **8** seine **9** ihr

3.3

A   **1** einen **2** sein **3** meine **4** unseren
    5 unser **6** ihre **7** meinen

B 1 der den 2 der 3 der der 4 der ein
5 den 6 ihren 7 ein

C 1 den Wein 2 die Trauben 3 die Körbe
4 das Auto 5 den Flaschöffner

3.4

A 1 ihrer 2 der 3 den 4 ihren
5 seiner 6 ihrer 7 ihren

B 1 den Arbeitern 2 den Helfern 3 den Nachbarn
4 den Mädchen 5 ihren Freundinnen Ansichtskarten
6 den Winzern

3.5 1 des Weines 2 der Familie 3 meiner Eltern
4 meines Bruders 5 deiner Vorfahren 6 dieser Stadt
7 des Sommers

3.6

A 1 Kunden 2 Kunde 3 dem Kunden 4 den Studenten
5 den Namen dieses Herrn 6 des Sachsen

B Karl und Elfriede haben ein Weingut in Alzey. Karl erzählt Susan von seiner
Arbeit und sie probieren den Wein. Karl und Elfriede arbeiten zusammen mit
der Winzergenossenschaft und sie verkaufen ihre Weine in alle Welt. Das
Weingut ist ein Familienbetrieb und alle Familienmitglieder helfen bei der
Weinlese. Susan und Carla finden einen Zeltplatz in der Nähe von Alzey
und sprechen mit einem Nachbarn. Carla kann den Flaschenöffner nicht
finden, er liegt bei ihren Klamotten!

Unit 4

4.1

A Elfriede wird dieses Jahr einundfünfzig Jahre alt.
Die Großmutter wird achtzig. Hans ist fast dreißig.
Die Großmutter ist neunundzwanzig Jahre älter als
Elfriede und fast fünfzig Jahre älter als Hans.

B 1 achttausendachthundertachtundvierzig
zweitausendneunhundertdreiundsechzig
dreitausendsiebenhundert
2 fünfzehnhundertsechsundachtzig zweihundert
3 achtzehnhundertzweiundneunzig (ein)hundert vierundvierzig
von neunzehnhundertfünfundvierzig bis
neunzehnhundertneunundachtzig
neunzehnhunderteinundneunzig fünfundzwanzig vierzehn

4.2   **1** erste **2** der Zweite **3** fünfzehnten
       4 einundzwanzigste **5** dreiundzwanzigsten

4.3

A   **1** ein Zwölftel **2** ein Zwanzigstel
     3 Hälfte **4** ein Fünfzehntel

B   **1** achtundzwanzig Komma fünf = ungefähr ein Drittel
     2 neunzehn Komma neun = ungefähr ein Fünftel
     3 sechzehn Komma drei = ungefähr ein Sechstel
     4 acht Komma eins = ungefähr ein Zwölftel

4.4   **1** neun Uhr zehn, zehn nach neun
       2 vierzehn Uhr fünfunddreißig, fünf nach halb drei (nachmittags)
       3 zwanzig Uhr siebenundfünfzig, drei Minuten vor neun (abends)
       4 elf Uhr fünfzehn, Viertel nach elf, viertel zwölf
       5 fünfzehn Uhr vierzig, zwanzig vor vier (nachmittags)
       6 null Uhr drei, drei Minuten nach zwölf Uhr nachts, drei
          Minuten nach Mitternacht
       7 zwölf Uhr fünfundzwanzig, fünf vor halb eins
       8 siebzehn Uhr fünfundvierzig, Viertel vor sechs (abends),
          drei viertel sechs (abends)
       9 zwölf Uhr siebzehn, siebzehn Minuten nach zwölf
     10 zwölf Uhr dreißig, halb eins
     11 neunzehn Uhr fünfundfünfzig, fünf Minuten vor acht (abends)
     12 siebzehn Uhr achtunddreißig, zweiundzwanzig Minuten vor
        sechs (abends)

4.5

A   **1** ersten ersten **2** sechsten ersten **3** elften elften
     4 elf Uhr elf **5** zweiundzwanzigsten dritten
     6 fünfundzwanzigsten vierten **7** ersten fünften
     8 siebzehnten sechsten **9** neunzehnhundertdreiundfünfzig
    10 dritten zehnten **11** einunddreißigsten zehnten
    12 ersten elften **13** zweiten elften **14** sechsten zwölften
    15 vierundzwanzigsten zwölften
    16 fünfundzwanzigste zwölfte
    17 sechsundzwanzigste zwölfte
    18 einunddreißigsten zwölften

B   **1** am zweiten Mai **2** am vierundzwanzigsten August
     3 am elften September **4** am zweiten Oktober
     5 der siebte Oktober **6** am achtzehnten Oktober
     7 am vierten November **8** am siebten November
     9 am neunten November

4.6

A   Zutaten: einhundertfünfzig Gramm Schokolade, einhundertfünfzig Gramm Butter, einhundertfünfzig Gramm Zucker, ein gestrichener Teelöffel Backpulver, sechs Eier, dreißig Gramm Puderzucker, einhundertfünfzig Gramm Mehl, Aprikosenkuvertüre

B   **1** zehn Äpfel **2** ein Glas Marmelade **3** eine Schachtel Pralinen
      4 zwei Pfund (ein Kilo) Kaffee **5** eine Flasche Wein

4.7

A   **1** Susan ist seit einer Woche in Frankfurt.
      2 Die Familie besitzt (hat) diesen Weinberg seit drei Generationen.
      3 Ich arbeite seit fünf Jahren bei Siemens.
      4 Die Großmutter lebt seit achtzig Jahren in Alzey.
      5 Ich trinke seit fünf Jahren keinen Kaffee.

B   **1** Tag für Tag **2** Jeden Tag **3** Heute Morgen
      4 Gestern Abend **5** heute Morgen **6** Diesmal
      7 In diesem Moment **8** Zum dritten Mal
      9 pünktlich **10** Zur Zeit

Unit 5

5.1

A   *(Possible answers)*
      1 against, into **2** around **3** anti (against) **4** around
      5 at **6** to **7** after **8** — **9** from **10** made of
      11 out of   out of

B   **1** nach **2** vor **3** an **4** in **5** für **6** bei **7** seit

5.2

A   **1** den **2** ihren **3** ihren **4** diese **5** die

B   **1** für ihre Mutter **2** für ihren Vater **3** für ihre Freundin
      4 für ihren Freund **5** für den Onkel in Birmingham
      6 für die Tante in Manchester

5.3

A   **1** Susan spricht mit der Dame.
      2 Susan spricht mit dem Kind.
      3 Susan spricht mit der Oma.

4 Susan spricht mit der Studentin.
5 Susan spricht mit dem Winzer.
6 Susan spricht mit seiner Frau.
7 Susan spricht mit dem Computerfachmann.
8 Susan spricht mit Herrn Gruber.
9 Roswitha erzählt ihr von ihrem Zimmer.
10 Roswitha erzählt ihr von dem Leben an der Uni.
11 Roswitha erzählt ihr von den Prüfungen.
12 Roswitha erzählt ihr von ihrem Freund.
13 Roswitha erzählt ihr von ihren Eltern.
14 Roswitha erzählt ihr von der Arbeit.
15 Roswitha erzählt ihr von der Universitätsbibliothek.
16 Roswitha erzählt ihr von ihrem Professor.

B   1 der 2 diesem 3 meinen 4 der 5 meinem 6 der

5.4

A   1 das 2 den 3 das 4 die 5 das
6 die 7 die 8 das 9 den 10 die

B   1 dem 2 dem 3 dem 4 der 5 dem
6 der 7 der 8 dem 9 dem 10 der

C   1 Ich hänge das Bild an die Wand.
2 Ich lege die Kissen auf das Sofa.
3 Ich stelle den Papierkorb unter den Tisch.
4 Ich stelle den Computer auf das Regal.
5 Ich stelle den Wecker auf das Schränkchen.
6 Ich stelle den Stuhl in den Garten.
7 Ich hänge den Mantel an die Tür.
8 Ich stelle den CD-Spieler auf das Schränkchen.
9 Ich werfe den Abfall auf den Boden.

D   1 Er steht auf dem Regal.
2 Sie stellt ihn auf das Regal.
3 Sie hängen in dem Kleiderschrank.
4 Sie hängt sie in den Kleiderschrank.
5 Sie steht auf dem Tisch.
6 Sie stellt sie auf den Tisch.
7 Sie geht gern in den Grünburgpark.
8 Sie sitzt gern in dem Grünburgpark.
9 Er hängt an der Wand.
10 Sie hängt ihn an die Wand.
11 Sie stellt ihn unter das Bett.
12 Er liegt unter dem Bett.
13 Er arbeitet in einem Büro.
14 Er geht in das Büro.

5.5

A   1 des Streiks 2 der Mittagspause 3 des Lärms
4 eines Briefes

B   1 der 2 meiner 3 meinen 4 Monaten 5 einigen
6 Wochen 7 einem 8 einer 9 der 10 unser 11 dem
12 der 13 des 14 Semesters 15 seinem 16 meinem
17 meiner 18 den 19 meinem

5.6

1 Susans Bruder geht aufs Gymnasium.
2 Roswitha stellt viele Sachen unters Bett.
3 Ich laufe schnell zur Post und kaufe Briefmarken.
4 Ich gehe zum Bahnhof und kaufe meine Fahrkarte.
5 Im Theater spielt morgen abend Shakespeares „Hamlet".

5.7

A   1 hinaus 2 herein 3 hinauf 4 herein 5 hinunter
6 hinaus

B   1 Wo ist das Buch? Dort (da) auf dem Tisch.
2 Ist Roswitha da? Ja, sie ist da (hier).
3 Hier (da) bin ich!
4 Wo ist der Drucker? Hier (da) unter dem Tisch.

5.8

1 Ich fahre gerne damit in die Stadt.
2 Ich wohne bei ihr.
3 Ich lege die Bücher darauf.
4 Daneben steht der Papierkorb.
5 Ich weiß nichts davon.
6 Ich habe einen Brief von ihm.

5.9

A   1 von der 2 an das 3 auf die 4 auf seine 5 mit einer
6 an ihre 7 auf den 8 um eine 9 für das 10 um
11 über das

B   1 an 2 von 3 in 4 Während 5 von 6 zu 7 bei
8 ins 9 im 10 in 11 nach 12 zum

Unit 6

6.1

A   1 In ganz Deutschland gibt es regionale Spezialitäten.
Regionale Spezialitäten gibt es in ganz Deutschland.
2 Mein Auto repariere ich selbst.

3 Meine Hosentasche flicke ich selbst.
4 Am liebsten esse ich Schokolade.
   Ich esse am liebsten Schokolade.
5 Jeden Morgen fährt Hans mit seinem Auto von Usingen nach Frankfurt zur Arbeit.
   Mit seinem Auto fährt Hans jeden Morgen von Usingen nach Frankfurt zur Arbeit.
   Von Usingen fährt Hans jeden Morgen mit seinem Auto nach Frankfurt zur Arbeit.
   Zur Arbeit fährt Hans jeden Morgen mit seinem Auto von Usingen nach Frankfurt.

B 1 In Köln feiert man Karneval.
2 In Mainz feiert man Fastnacht.
3 In München feiert man Fasching.
4 Im Dreiländereck zwischen Freiburg, Basel und Straßburg feiert man Fasnet.

C 1 Oft bekomme ich einen Brief mit einem Problem.
2 Meistens ist das nicht so einfach.
3 Zwischendurch klingelt das Telefon.
4 Dann unterbreche ich die Arbeit.
5 Danach beginne ich wieder von Anfang an.
6 Außerdem gibt es noch viele Probleme vom Vortag.
7 Am besten lege ich alle Probleme in den Aktenschrank.
8 Dann trinke ich eine Tasse Kaffee.

6.2

A 1 Ich kann nächste Woche nach Frankfurt fahren.
2 Ich habe eine neue Jacke gekauft.
3 Er wird morgen nach Bad Dürkheim fahren.
4 Roswitha hat ein schönes Kostüm für die Fastnacht gekauft.
5 Dieter lernt Susan und Jane kennen.
6 Hans kann sehr viel von der Fastnacht erzählen.
7 Susan muss eine neue Bluse kaufen.
8 Roswitha möchte ihre Familie in Alzey besuchen.
9 Susan kann das Loch in der Hose flicken.

B 1 Im Sommer gehe ich im See schwimmen.
2 Im Winter laufe ich gern Ski.
3 Meine Schwester geht jeden Sonntag im Reitstadion reiten.
4 Wir gehen in ein sehr schönes Restaurant essen.
5 Im Schwarzwald gehe ich gern spazieren.
6 In der Turnhalle gehe ich ab und zu turnen.*
7 Wir spielen auf dem Sportplatz gern Tennis.

*Note: No. 6 above could also be **in die Turnhalle** if the speaker is thinking more of going *to* the gym rather than the exercises done *in* the gym.

6.3

A
1 Susan fährt nach Bad Dürkheim mit.
2 Abends sehen die Kinder fern.
3 Wir kommen erst um 21 Uhr in Bad Dürkheim an.
4 In Sachsen steht man sehr früh auf.
5 In Frankfurt steigt man oft um.

B
1 The doctor writes me a prescription for some tablets.
2 That is not a mistake, I have only made a slip of the pen.
3 The student copies the correct answer from his friend.
4 The head of department signs the letter.
5 The company has put the new project out to tender.
6 We have been given new instructions.

C
1 erzählen 2 entdecken missverstehen 3 versuchen
4 empfiehlt 5 besucht

D *You will probably have had to check most of these in a dictionary.*
1 sitzen bleiben (*two verbs*)
2 Ski fahren (*noun plus verb*)
3 fallen lassen (*two verbs*)
4 zurückgeben (*prefix is a preposition*)
5 voll stopfen (*adjective plus verb*)
6 vollenden (*meaning of adjective is no longer evident, hence one word*)
7 schief gehen (*adverb plus verb*)
8 wieder erkennen (*adverb plus verb*)

6.4

A
1 Ich fahre jeden Morgen um 7 Uhr mit dem Auto zur Arbeit.
2 Die Fastnacht feiert man jedes Jahr in vielen Teilen Deutschlands.
3 Hans frühstückt jeden Morgen um 8 Uhr zu Hause.
4 Roswitha geht jeden Morgen um 8 Uhr zu Fuß zur Universität.
5 Letztes Jahr bin ich mit dem Auto nach Deutschland gefahren.
6 Samstags fahre ich gern mit meiner Familie nach Frankfurt einkaufen.
7 Susan wird nächstes Jahr wieder nach Deutschland kommen.
8 Der Zug kommt pünktlich auf Gleis 3 an.
9 Nächste Woche fährt Dieter mit dem Auto nach Italien auf Urlaub.
10 Carlas Mutter fährt schnell in die Stadt einkaufen.

B
1 Sie schenkt ihrer Mutter ein Buch.
Sie schenkt ihr ein Buch.
Sie schenkt es ihrer Mutter.
Sie schenkt es ihr.
2 Er zeigt Susan die Stadt Frankfurt.
Er zeigt ihr die Stadt Frankfurt.
Er zeigt sie Susan.
Er zeigt sie ihr.

    3 Sie schreibt ihren Eltern einen Brief.
       Sie schreibt ihnen einen Brief.
       Sie schreibt ihn ihren Eltern.
       Sie schreibt ihn ihnen.

6.5

A

1. Isst man in England wirklich am Fastnachtsdienstag Pfannkuchen?
2. Isst man in Thüringen wirklich Thüringer Klöße?
3. Ist am Aschermittwoch die Fastnacht wirklich vorbei?
4. Trinkt man in Bayern wirklich sehr viel Bier?
5. Fährt der Sonderzug Pappnase wirklich nur in der Karnevalszeit?
6. Feiert man in Südamerika wirklich auch Karneval?
7. Gibt es am Rosenmontag wirklich einen großen Umzug in Köln?
8. Flickt Susan wirklich das Loch in der Hosentasche?
9. Bezahlen Roswitha und Susan wirklich ihr Bier selbst?
10. Nimmt Dieter wirklich nicht zu?

B

1. Wie heißt der Zug?
2. Wann fährt der Zug?
3. Woher kommt der Zug?
4. Wohin fährt der Zug?
5. Was für ein Zug ist er?
6. Wer führt den Hund spazieren?
7. Wann führt Hans seinen Hund spazieren?
8. Wo führt Hans den Hund spazieren?
9. Wie lange führt Hans seinen Hund spazieren?
10. Wie viele Menschen strömen jedes Jahr ins Rheinland, um den Karnevalszug in Köln zu sehen?
11. Was möchten die Menschen sehen?
12. Warum strömen tausende Menschen jährlich ins Rheinland?
13. Was wird verliehen?
14. Wo wird der Orden verliehen?
15. Wem wird er verliehen?
16. Wie viel Schokolade isst Susan?
17. Warum isst Susan Schokolade?

6.6

1. Ich kaufe keine Schokolade.
2. Wir gehen morgen nicht.
3. Wir gehen morgen nicht in den Zoo.
4. Er wohnt nicht in Frankfurt.
5. Er hat kein Auto.
6. Er fährt nicht mit dem Auto in die Stadt.
7. Hier darf man nicht parken.

Unit 7

7.1

1 Ich habe viele Bücher gekauft.
2 Ich habe an der Humboldt-Universität studiert.
3 Ich habe Russisch gelernt.
4 Ich habe in Berlin gewohnt.
5 Ich habe ein Zimmer in einem Studentenwohnheim gehabt.
6 Ich habe das Zimmer jede Woche aufgeräumt.
7 Die Fahrt mit der U-Bahn hat 20 Pfennig gekostet.
8 Ich habe viel gearbeitet.
9 Ich habe nicht viel über Politik geredet.

7.2

1 Susan hat zwei Wochen bei Carla gewohnt.
2 Susan hat einen Brief an ihre Eltern geschrieben.
3 Ich habe die U-Bahn an der Hauptwache genommen.
4 Die Oma in Alzey hat trotz ihres Alters schwere Körbe gehoben.
5 Rüdiger hat ein Zimmer in Frankfurt gemietet.
6 Carla hat ihren Flaschenöffner nicht gefunden.
7 Auf der Geburtstagsfeier haben sie viel Wein getrunken.
8 Roswitha und Herr Schulz haben über die Vergangenheit gesprochen.
9 Susan hat Herrn Schulz auf dem Campingplatz getroffen.
10 Roswitha hat lange geschlafen.
11 Bei der Weinlese haben die Familienmitglieder geholfen.
12 Der Film hat um acht Uhr begonnen.

7.3

A
1 ist gefahren 2 ist gegangen 3 ist gewesen
4 ist aufgestanden 5 ist angekommen 6 bin geblieben
7 ist gekommen 8 bin geblieben

B
1 hat 2 ist 3 hat 4 habe 5 ist
6 ist 7 hat 8 ist 9 ist 10 hat

C
Von Tschernobyl hast du bestimmt gehört. Aber kurz darauf ist in einem Chemiewerk in der Schweiz ein Feuer ausgebrochen. Davon hat man damals viel in den Zeitungen gelesen. Viele chemische Giftstoffe sind in den Rhein gekommen. Viele Fische sind gestorben. Man hat die toten Fische aus dem Rhein gefischt. Alle haben sich fürchterlich über das Unglück aufgeregt. Die Firma hat man später freigesprochen. Kurz darauf ist ein anderes Unglück am Main passiert. Wieder sind viele Giftstoffe in den Rhein geflossen. In Spanien ist der Inhalt eines mit Schwermetallen verschmutzten Sammelbeckens ausgelaufen und hat das Naturschutzgebiet Doñana vergiftet. Das gleiche ist in Rumänien geschehen.

Das Unglück in Tschernobyl ist vor vielen Jahren geschehen und das Gebiet ist heute noch radioaktiv verseucht, der Rhein hat sich zum Teil erneuert und selbst die Ölverschmutzung an der Atlantikküste ist allmählich verschwunden. Aber wie lange können wir die Umwelt ohne nachhaltige Folgen für Menschen, Tiere und Pflanzen verschmutzen?

7.4

A

1 Susan fuhr nach Frankfurt.
2 Susan ging mit Hans ins Kino.
3 Rüdiger war sehr fleißig.
4 Roswitha stand um sieben Uhr auf.
5 Der Bus kam um 17 Uhr am Hauptbahnhof an.
6 Gestern abend blieb ich zu Hause.
7 Herr Schulz kam nach der Wende nach Frankfurt.
8 Ich blieb nicht lange in der Disko.

1 Susan trank auf der Geburtstagsfeier viel Wein.
2 Susan fuhr nach Deutschland.
3 Hans kaufte einen Opel.
4 Ich machte einen Fehler.
5 Der Chef flog von London nach Frankfurt.
6 Herr Schulz blieb nach der Wende nicht lange in Berlin.
7 Auf der Geburtstagsfeier tanzte Hans mit Susan.
8 Hans war noch nie in England.
9 Aber er flog einmal nach Amerika.
10 Susan lernte schon als Baby schwimmen.

B Wer gestern aus dem Fenster schaute, konnte am Wetter irre werden; Schnee, Regen, dann wieder Sonnenschein. Drei Tage vor dem 1. Mai kam der Winter noch einmal zurück. Selbst im Rheinland sanken die Temperaturen wieder unter den Gefrierpunkt. Allein die Autobahnwache Hagen registrierte innerhalb weniger Stunden elf typische Winter-Unfälle. München versank in dichtem Schneetreiben. Auch in England gab es zum Teil heftige Schneefälle. Im Schneesturm stürzte eine Privatmaschine nördlich von London ab. Die vier Insassen aus Holland kamen ums Leben. Südlich von Plymouth sank ein Fischkutter; ein Flugzeugträger rettete die fünfköpfige Besatzung.

7.5

So schlecht war das Leben in der alten DDR auch nicht. Wir kannten keine Arbeitslosen, wir hatten billige Grundlebensmittel und man konnte billig mit dem Bus oder mit dem Zug fahren. Natürlich durften wir aber nicht reisen. Das empfanden wir alle sehr negativ. Bücher waren billig. Man konnte halt nur nicht alle Bücher kaufen. Ich studierte Mathematik, in naturwissenschaftlichen Fächern spürte man am wenigsten Politik. Wir diskutierten natürlich auch politische Themen, aber eben nicht so viel wie in den Geisteswissenschaften.

7.6

A

1 Er war in Leipzig zur Schule gegangen.
2 Er war bei den Pionieren gewesen.
3 Er hatte für die U-Bahn nur 20 Pfennige bezahlt.
4 Er war oft mit der U-Bahn gefahren.
5 Er war überall herumgefahren.
6 Er hatte einen Studienplatz bekommen.
7 Er hatte in Berlin studiert.

B

1 Ungarn hatte die Grenze nach Österreich geöffnet.
2 In Leipzig hatten 20 000 Menschen demonstriert.
3 Eine große Militärparade hatte stattgefunden.
4 Der Staatsratsvorsitzende war zurückgetreten.
5 Die größte Demonstration hatte am 4. November stattgefunden.
6 Die Regierung war am 7. November zurückgetreten.

Unit 8

8.1

A

1 Ich will nach York gehen.
2 Dort kann man auch Linguistik studieren.
3 Ich soll auch mit Computern arbeiten.
4 Ich muss tüchtig lernen.
5 Vielleicht kann ich auf dem Gebiet der Maschinen-
übersetzung arbeiten.
6 Das soll sehr interessant sein.
7 Ich möchte nächstes Jahr wieder nach Deutschland kommen.
8 Ich kann vielleicht Übersetzerin werden.
9 Ich möchte für eine große Firma arbeiten.
10 Ich kann auch freiberuflich arbeiten.

B

1 Er muss aber lernen.
2 Sie muss aber Briefe schreiben.
3 Wir müssen uns aber umweltfreundlich verhalten.
4 Du musst aber eine Stelle finden.
5 Ihr müsst aber viel arbeiten.
6 Sie müssen sich aber Gedanken über die Zukunft machen.

C

1 Ich konnte Deutschland besuchen.
2 Ich durfte ins Kino gehen.
3 Ich sollte mehr Grammatik lernen.
4 Er musste seine Hausaufgaben machen.
5 Sie wollte ein neues Kleid kaufen.

8.2

A

1 Roswitha schreibt an viele Firmen um sich um eine Stelle zu bewerben.
2 Hans besucht Leipzig um die Lage dort zu sehen.

3 Die Freunde treffen sich in Roswithas Zimmer um miteinander zu sprechen

4 Ich fliege nach Berlin um schneller anzukommen.

5 Ich kaufe eine Zeitung um sie im Flugzeug zu lesen.

6 Sie wählen zuerst 00 49 69 um Frankfurt von England aus direkt zu wählen.

7 Roswitha lernt viel um ein gutes Examen zu machen.

8 Hans macht Überstunden um Geld für seinen Urlaub zu sparen.

9 Die Freunde fahren nach Bad Dürkheim um Susan den Wurstmarkt zu zeigen.

10 Hans trifft Carla auf der Hauptwache um mit ihr ins Kino zu gehen.

B
1 Die Nummer ist im Telefonbuch nicht zu finden.
2 Herr Beck ist unter einer anderen Nummer zu erreichen.
3 Das ist heute nicht zu machen.
4 Das ist nicht zu glauben.

C
1 Hast du Lust eine Radtour zu machen?
2 Hast du Lust auf den Wurstmarkt nach Bad Dürkheim zu fahren?
3 Hast du Lust heute abend ins Kino zu gehen?
4 Hast du Lust die Geburtstagsgeschenke aufzumachen?

8.3

Possible answers:
1 möchte 2 will 3 wird 4 will 5 möchte 6 wird

8.4

A
1 Ich würde in einem schönen Hotel wohnen.
2 Ich würde in der Sonne liegen.
3 Ich würde Moussaka essen und Wein trinken.
4 Ich würde eine Insel besuchen.
5 Ich würde alte Freunde treffen.

B
1 Ich wünschte, ich wäre auf Urlaub.
2 Ich wünschte, ich hätte ein schönes Haus.
3 Ich wünschte, ich würde in der Sonne liegen.
4 Ich wünschte, ich könnte viel essen und trinken.
5 Ich wünschte, ich könnte mitfahren.
6 Ich wünschte, ich würde am Strand stehen.
7 Ich wünschte, ich müsste nie nach Hause fahren.

8.5

1 If she were ill I would have to come alone.
2 If I had learned more at school I would be able to go to university now.
3 If I were as hard-working as my brother I could be an engineer.
4 If I had known of the party I would have come along .
5 If he were not to come tomorrow we would have to celebrate without him.
6 If only you were here we could celebrate together.

Unit 9

9.1

A   1 sich   2 mich   3 sich   4 sich   5 euch
        6 uns   7 sich   8 mir   9 dir

B   1 sich   2 sich   3 uns   4 uns   5 uns

9.2

A   1 Viel Bier wird getrunken.
        2 Die Zeitung wird gelesen.
        3 Der Rock wird genäht.
        4 Ein Auto wird gemietet.
        5 Das Hotelzimmer wird reserviert.
        6 Ein Telegramm wird auch geschickt.

B   1 Die Adresse wird auf den Umschlag geschrieben.
        2 Der Absender wird auf die Rückseite geschrieben.
        3 Der Brief wird in den Umschlag gesteckt.
        4 Er wird zum Briefkasten getragen.
        5 Er wird in den Briefkasten gesteckt.
        6 Alle Briefe werden vom Briefkasten abgeholt.
        7 Sie werden zur Post gefahren.
        8 Die Briefe werden dort automatisch sortiert.
        9 Die Briefe werden an den Zustellungsort geschickt.
      10 Sie werden zugestellt.
      11 Mein Brief wird aus dem Briefkasten geholt.
      12 Der Brief wird gelesen und eine Antwort geschrieben.

9.3

A   1 Am 26. Mai 1952 wurde die Grenze BRD-DDR abgeriegelt.
        2 Am 24. Juli 1952 wurden die fünf Länder in der DDR aufgelöst.
        3 Am 13. August 1961 wurde die Berliner Mauer gebaut.
        4 Am 2. Mai 1989 wurde begonnen, die Grenze Ungarn-
          Österreich abzubauen.
        5 Am 9. November 1989 wurden die Grenzen in Deutschland
          geöffnet.
        6 Am 1. Juli 1990 wurde die D-Mark in der DDR eingeführt.
        7 Am 3. Oktober 1990 wurde Deutschland wieder vereinigt.

B   1 Neue Telefonanschlüsse wurden allmählich geschaffen.
        2 Die Arbeitslosen wurden allmählich wieder eingestellt.
        3 Die Häuser wurden allmählich repariert.
        4 Die Lehrer wurden allmählich umgeschult.
        5 Die Renten wurden allmählich erhöht.
        6 Die Arbeitszeit wurde allmählich angeglichen.

C   1 wird ... angebaut   2 wurden ... bearbeitet   3 wurden ... zerstört
         4 wurde ... angebaut   5 wird ... abgefüllt   6 wird ... exportiert
         7 wird ... getrunken   8 wurde ... ausgezeichnet   9 wird ... verkauft
       10 wird ... produziert

D   1 von meiner   2 mit der   3 mit   4 mit   5 von der   6 durch ein

9.4

A   *Possible answers:*
       1 There was dancing until midnight.
       2 In England it's not done like that.
       3 It's time to go to sleep now.
       4 We'll have stew tomorrow.
       5 There were a lot of people in the street.

B   1 Um 8.30 Uhr wird geduscht.
       2 Mein Frühstück wird gegessen.
       3 Es wird zur Arbeit gefahren.
       4 Die Post wird gelesen.
       5 Die Briefe werden diktiert.
       6 Um 12 Uhr wird Mittagspause gemacht.
       7 Es wird in ein Restaurant gegangen.
       8 Es wird gut gegessen.
       9 Ein Bericht wird geschrieben.
      10 Es wird nach Hause gegangen.

9.5

A   1 Ich lasse den Automechaniker mein Auto reparieren.
       2 Ich lasse den Elektriker unseren Toaster reparieren.
       3 Ich lasse meine Schwester meinen Computer reparieren.
       4 Ich lasse die Sekretärin den Brief schreiben.
       5 Ich lasse den Maler das Zimmer tapezieren.
       6 Ich lasse meine Mutter das Kleid nähen.
       7 Ich lasse den Friseur die Haare schneiden.
       8 Ich lasse meinen Sohn das Essen machen.
       9 Ich lasse die Spülmaschine das Geschirr abwaschen.
      10 Ich lasse den Gärtner den Rasen mähen.
      11 Ich lasse den Klempner die Wasserleitung reparieren.

B   *Possible answers:*
       1 He kept me waiting.
       2 That cannot be denied.
       3 Leave me in peace!
       4 The boss had the head of department called in.
       5 I will not put up with that.
       6 I'll have it brought at once.

9.6
1 Man sortiert die Post automatisch.
2 Hier darf man nicht rauchen.
3 Man verstaatlichte die Firma.
4 Man hat das System verbessert.
5 Man schaffte Inlandstelegramme ab.

Unit 10

10.1

A
1 warm 2 laut 3 klein 4 dumm 5 froh 6 alt
7 langweilig 8 altmodisch 9 langsam 10 billig

B
Possible answers:
1 gelb 2 teuer 3 unbequem 4 alt 5 laut
6 ungewohnt

10.2
1 kalte 2 roten 3 Londoner 4 alte nett 5 alten
6 großen 7 neue 8 alten 9 neue 10 neuen

10.3
1 schicken 2 schwarze roten 3 schwarze 4 weißes
5 elegantes 6 schönen modischen 7 elegante
8 schöne neues 9 schönen neuen goldene
10 schwarzen losen breiten

10.4
1 mein deiner 2 meine deine 3 ein eins 4 ein keins
5 dein meiner 6 ihres seins

10.5
1 umfassende 2 spielendes 3 gekochtes 4 führende
5 gestohlenes 6 strahlend

10.6
Possible answers:
1 gut 2 oft schnell 3 gern 4 ruhig weiter 5 sehr

10.7
Possible answers:
1 Du kennst doch meinen Bruder!
2 Trink doch noch eine Tasse Tee.
3 Und wo kommst du denn her?
4 Das Kleid ist ja teuer!
5 Kleider kosten eben viel Geld.
6 Komm doch mit!

10.8
1 Das Auto ist schneller als die Straßenbahn, aber der Zug ist
am schnellsten.
2 Jazz ist besser als Popmusik, aber klassische Musik ist am besten.

3 Der Praktikant ist fleißiger als ich, aber der Chef ist am fleißigsten.
4 Die Alpen sind höher als der Westerwald, aber der Himalaya ist am höchsten.
5 Elfriede ist älter als Hans, aber Oma ist am ältesten.
6 Elfriede ist jünger als Oma, aber Hans ist am jüngsten.
7 Das Frühjahr ist wärmer als der Winter, aber der Sommer ist am wärmsten.
8 Eine Minute ist kürzer als eine Stunde, aber eine Sekunde ist am kürzesten.
9 Das Christentum ist älter als der Islam, aber der Judaismus ist am ältesten.
10 Hans schläft länger als Roswitha, aber Dieter schläft am längsten.
11 Wurst schmeckt besser als Käse, aber Kuchen schmeckt am besten.
12 Mit dem Zug fahren ist umweltfreundlicher als mit dem Auto, aber zu Fuß gehen ist am umweltfreundlichsten.

10.9

A
1 „Der Alte" ist eine bekannte deutsche Fernsehsendung.
2 Die Firma hat 200 Angestellte.
3 Er ist Angestellter bei Siemens.
4 Sie hat mir etwas Interessantes erzählt.
5 Mein Bekannter wohnt in München.

B
1 neue 2 schönes 3 große 4 vielen 5 schönen
6 verschiedene 7 gelben 8 breiten 9 enge 10 schicke
11 elegantes 12 gelbe 13 empfindlich 14 breite
15 altmodisch 16 enge 17 schicke 18 teuer 19 elegante
20 alt 21 wohl 22 alten 23 Neues

C
1 alt 2 lange 3 führende 4 deutschen 5 größte
6 deutsche 7 Ersten 8 neue 9 Weimarer
10 mittelalterlichen 11 malerischen 12 Thüringer
13 schönsten 14 unverdorbensten 15 ausgedehnten
16 sprudelnden 17 blühenden

Unit 11

11.1
1 Carla kommt nicht aus England, sondern sie kommt aus Deutschland.
2 Meistens trinke ich Tee, aber manchmal trinke ich Kaffee.
3 Ich kann das Kleid nicht kaufen, denn ich habe kein Geld.
4 Dieter geht zu Fuß, denn er hat kein Auto.
5 Sie sind nicht ins Kino gegangen, sondern haben einen Spaziergang gemacht.
6 Trinken Sie ein Glas Bier oder möchten Sie eine Tasse Kaffee?
7 Er ist mit dem Taxi gefahren, denn er hatte keine Zeit.

8 Ich habe eine Fahrkarte gekauft und bin nach München gefahren.

9 Jeder möchte gerne lernen, denn jeder möchte beruflich weiterkommen.

10 Mein Bruder hat einen praktischen Beruf gelernt und möchte jetzt studieren.

11.2

A

1 Wir wissen schon, dass die Schule nicht weit vom Haus ist.
2 Wir wissen schon, dass die erste Stunde um 7.50 Uhr beginnt.
3 Wir wissen schon, dass sie nachmittags Schulaufgaben macht.
4 Wir wissen schon, dass sie später eine Freundin besucht.
5 Wir wissen schon, dass sie Musik hören.
6 Wir wissen schon, dass sie abends meistens zu Hause bleibt.
7 Wir wissen schon, dass sie selten Briefe schreibt.

B

1 Wir kaufen dieses Kleid, weil es billig ist.
2 Roswitha lernt viel, weil sie ein gutes Examen machen möchte.
3 Wir können nicht ausgehen, weil wir kein Geld haben.
4 Roswitha bewirbt sich um eine Stelle, weil sie einen Arbeitsplatz sucht.
5 Dieters Bruder studiert, weil er seine Berufsaussichten verbessern möchte.
6 Ich trinke viel Limonade, weil es sehr heiß ist.
7 Roswitha fährt nach Alzey, weil sie ihre Eltern besuchen möchte.
8 Dieter weiß vom Projekt bei Lucas, weil er es in der Zeitung gelesen hat.
9 Dieter liest die Zeitung, weil er sich informieren möchte.
10 Hans geht zu Fuß, weil das Auto in der Werkstatt ist.

11.3

A

1 Die Bluse ist für ihre Schwester, die noch zur Schule geht.
2 Die Flasche ist für ihren Vater, der gern Wein trinkt.
3 Der Schal ist für ihre Oma, die fünfundsiebzig ist.
4 Die Zigarren sind für ihren Onkel, der gern raucht.
5 Die Schokolade ist für ihre kleine Schwester, die alles Süße isst.
6 Die Krawatte ist für ihren Vetter, der in Leicester wohnt.
7 Der Teller ist für ihre Freundin, die nicht nach Deutschland fahren konnte.
8 Das Plakat ist für die Deutschlehrerin, die sehr nett ist.
9 Das Kuchenrezept ist für ihre Mutter, die gern Kuchen bäckt.
10 Der Bierkrug ist für ihren Freund, der sie von der Schule abholt.

B

1 die 2 die 3 das 4 der 5 die 6 dem 7 deren
8 dessen 9 deren 10 den

C

1 Das Geld, das auf dem Tisch liegt, ist für die Miete.
2 Die Studenten, die an der Haltestelle stehen, warten auf die Straßenbahn.

3 Der Computer, den Roswitha gekauft hat, ist sehr modern.
4 Die Stereoanlage, die ich in einem Schaufenster gesehen habe, ist sehr teuer.
5 Die Wirtin, bei der Roswitha wohnt, ist sehr nett.
6 Der Mann, dessen Frau krank ist, tut mir leid.
7 Der Student, dessen Auto kaputt ist, ruft die Werkstatt an.
8 Meine Freunde, denen ich gestern geschrieben habe, wohnen in München.
9 Die Bücher, die ich mir geliehen habe, sind sehr interessant.
10 Die Engländerin, die bei unseren Freunden war, war sehr nett.

11.4
1 Ich weiß nicht, ob Hans eine Freundin hat.
2 Ich weiß nicht, wann der Film beginnt.
3 Ich weiß nicht, ob das eine positive Entwicklung ist.
4 Ich weiß nicht, wie hoch die Zugspitze ist.
5 Ich weiß nicht, wie alt Roswitha ist.
6 ich weiß nicht, ob sie Geschwister hat.
7 Ich weiß nicht, wie lange sie schon studiert.
8 Ich weiß nicht, was Dieter später werden möchte.
9 Ich weiß nicht, ob Roswithas Eltern auch studiert haben.
10 Ich weiß nicht, wann Roswitha fertig wird.

11.5
1 Obwohl Dieter nicht viel Zeit hat, geht er mit Roswitha in die Kneipe.
2 Nachdem Susan gegessen hat, ruft sie ihre Eltern an.
3 Weil der Wurstmarkt sehr bekannt ist, fahren die Studenten nach Bad Dürkheim.
4 Als ich acht Jahre alt war, lernte ich Fahrrad fahren.
5 Als ich 17 Jahre alt war, fuhr ich zum ersten Mal nach Deutschland.
6 Weil Dieter sich informieren will, liest er viele Zeitungen.
7 Weil die weiße Bluse so teuer ist, kauft Susan sie nicht.
8 Dass jeder zehnte Brite eine Weiterbildung gemacht hat, stand in der Zeitung.
9 Wenn es sehr heiß ist, trinke ich viel Limonade.
10 Dass es ein neues Projekt gibt, habe ich schon in der Zeitung gelesen.

Unit 12

12.1
1 Sie sagt, dass man den Wald roden muss.
2 Sie sagt, dass das Tierleben gefährdet wird.
3 Sie sagt, dass die neue Straße direkt über den Wildpfad von Hirschen und Rehen führt.
4 Sie sagt, dass der Staat einen Zuschuss bewilligt hat.
5 Sie sagt, dass die Besiedlung des Berges das Wasser der Mineralquelle verunreinigt.

12.2

A

1 Man müsse den Wald roden.
2 Das Tierleben werde gefährdet.
3 Die neue Straße führe direkt über den Wildpfad von Hirschen und Rehen.
4 Der Staat habe einen Zuschuss bewilligt.
5 Die Besiedlung des Berges verunreinige das Wasser der Mineralquelle.

B

Ich war auf der Vorfahrtstraße. Plötzlich kam ein Auto aus der Seitenstraße. Es kann nicht gehalten haben, denn es kam zu schnell aus der Seitenstraße. Ich habe geschrien und auf die Bremse getreten, aber trotzdem bin ich auf das Auto geprallt. Dann lag ich auf der Straße. Der Autofahrer hat mitten auf der Straße angehalten. Ich stand unter Schock und habe versucht, aufzustehen. Das Fahrrad war kaputt, das Auto hat nur Blechschaden erlitten.

12.3

1 Roswitha und Susan haben gesagt: „Wir gehen einkaufen".
2 Herr Schulz hat gesagt: „Ich komme aus Sachsen und habe in Berlin studiert. Jetzt wohne ich in Frankfurt. Ich unterrichte Mathematik dort. Mein Bruder und meine Schwester wohnen in Leipzig, aber sie kommen oft nach Frankfurt."
3 Der Chefarzt behauptete: „Der Berg ist die idealste Lage für die Klinik. Ich habe in einer ähnlichen Klinik in Österreich gearbeitet; dort waren die Patienten aus aller Welt sehr zufrieden. Die gute Luft und die Möglichkeit, Spaziergänge zu unternehmen, beschleunigen die Genesung der Patienten."

12.4

1 „Frau Meyer, bitte reservieren Sie die Hotelzimmer."
2 „Herr Reinhard, bitte unterschreiben Sie die Briefe."
3 „Frau Müller, bitte machen Sie die Post auf."
4 „Frau Neumann, bitte ordnen Sie die Akten ein."
5 „Frau Wilhelm, bitte sortieren Sie die Rechnungen."

Index